ORDINARY
LOGIC

ORDINARY LOGIC

Robert H. Ennis
Cornell University

PRENTICE-HALL, INC., *Englewood Cliffs, N. J.*

I dedicate this book
to clear and critical thinking
wherever it appears.

PRENTICE-HALL, INTERNATIONAL, INC., *London*
PRENTICE-HALL OF AUSTRALIA, PTY. LTD., *Sydney*
PRENTICE-HALL OF CANADA, LTD., *Toronto*
PRENTICE-HALL OF INDIA PRIVATE LTD., *New Delhi*
PRENTICE-HALL OF JAPAN, INC., *Tokyo*

Preface to the Instructor

The writing of this book is based upon experience in teaching logic to students of all ages. It is a practical book written from the "ordinary language" point of view: Technical terminology and symbolism are kept to a practical minimum, rote-memory rules are avoided, and counter-intuitive interpretations of logical operators are not advocated.

This ordinary language approach to logic, in particular, does not accept the material implication interpretation of the 'if-then' operator, nor does it accept the inclusive interpretation of alternation. Instead, it holds that there is an implied connection between propositions joined by these operators. Furthermore, the ordinary language approach avoids the extensional interpretation of class logic (which parallels the material implication interpretation of 'if-then'). The merits and demerits of this ordinary language approach are argued in the philosophical literature (see the bibliography for some references), so I do little more than sketch out some of the major points in this book, which after all is not on the philosophy of logic.

The title, *Ordinary Logic*, signifies not only the ordinary language approach to logic, but also a concern with the everyday reasoning that people actually do. To the extent that people will need to know about them in the reasoning that they actually do, the two standard topics of introductory logic books, sentence and class reasoning, are covered in this book. One thing that other logic books barely or do not do, but which is done in this book, is to suggest how to apply the principles of logic to realistic situations.

For many students the presentation of logic in this book has been found to be self-teaching. The frequent sets of exercises to which answers are provided make it usable much like a programmed text. For other students, however, considerable help by an instructor is required, such help often taking the form of the presentation and consideration of more examples.

Local and contemporary examples presented either by students or instructor are helpful, but one must beware of examples that confuse by introducing problems not yet discussed. For instance, when securing examples to show that the general move from a statement to its converse is invalid, one must make sure that the converse of the statement is not true. Otherwise, many students are confused. The distinction between truth and validity is often slow in coming. In the study of class reasoning, to cite another instance, beware of the early introduction of examples that require a student to realize that the circle drawn outside in order to represent class inclusion might sometimes be made co-extensive. (See "Extent of the predicate class" near the end of Chapter 4.)

As with any textual presentation of any subject matter, I have omitted a number of qualifications, and urge you to add qualifications as time and student sophistication permit.

R. H. E.

Contents

CHAPTER 1 **Introduction**   1

CHAPTER 2 **Basic Ideas**   7

   Some Basic Terms   8
   Truth and Validity   9
   Emphasis on Criteria   10
  ∨ *Types of Deductive Reasoning*   11
   Chapter Summary   12
       COMPREHENSION SELF-TEST, 12

CHAPTER 3 **Sentence Reasoning**   13

  ∨ *Conditional Reasoning*   13
      The antecedent and the consequent, 14   The four basic forms, 14
         COMPREHENSION SELF-TEST, 16
      Order of premises, 18   The converse, 19   The contrapositive, 19   Double negation, 20
         COMPREHENSION SELF-TEST, 20
      Putting an argument in shape, 22   Using symbols to represent sentences, 25
         COMPREHENSION SELF-TEST, 28
      Necessary and/or sufficient conditions, 30   Only if, 33   The biconditional: if, and only if, 35   A conditional chain, 37
         COMPREHENSION SELF-TEST, 40

Other Major Types of Sentence Reasoning   42
> Reasoning using the conjunction 'and', 42   Negajunction:
> 'not-both' reasoning, 43   Alternation: 'either-or'
> reasoning, 44
>> COMPREHENSION SELF-TEST, 47

❖Greater Complexities   48
> ❖Step-by-step organization of arguments, 49
>> COMPREHENSION SELF-TEST, 51
> ❖Complex sentences, 51   ❖Indirect proof, 55   ❖Proving
> a conditional, 56
>> COMPREHENSION SELF-TEST, 57
> ❖Material implication, 59

Chapter Summary   62

CHAPTER 4   Class Reasoning   64

A Simple Euler Circle System   66
> General strategy, 68
>> COMPREHENSION SELF-TEST, 69
> Invalidity, 70
>> COMPREHENSION SELF-TEST, 71
> Negatives, 71   Transformations among negatives and
> positives, 72
>> COMPREHENSION SELF-TEST, 75
> Partial inclusion, 76   Ambiguity of 'some', 76   'At least
> some', 77   'Some but not all', 78   Partial exclusion, 79
>> COMPREHENSION SELF-TEST, 80
> Multiple premises, 81
>> COMPREHENSION SELF-TEST, 83
> Other interpretation problems, 83   Extent of the predicate
> class, 84
>> COMPREHENSION SELF-TEST, 87

Combination of Class and Sentence Reasoning   87
> Part-by-part use of the two systems, 88   Instantiation, 89
>> COMPREHENSION SELF-TEST, 90

Chapter Summary   91

CHAPTER 5   Practical Application of Deductive Logic   93

Looseness of Reasoning   93
> Step 1: the shift into idealized form, 94   Step 2:
> judgment of validity, 96   Step 3: the shift from the
> conclusion back to the world of reality, 96   Summary, 100

Other Types of Deduction   100
> Mathematics, 100   Alethic logic, 101   Deontic logic, 101
> Epistemic logic, 101   Spatial logic, 101   Other types, 101

Examples of Practical Reasoning in More Detail   102
> An aspect of the frontier thesis, 102   Supply and demand,
> 108   Neoclassical English writing, 111   A body immersed in
> a fluid, 113

Chapter Summary   116

       COMPREHENSION SELF-TEST, 117

Suggested Further Reading in Logic   118

Answers   **120**

Index   **149**

ORDINARY LOGIC

CHAPTER 1

Introduction

The purpose of this book is to help a person unacquainted with logic to grasp the useful features of two basic types of logic; to come to understand what counts as a deductive proof; and to see applications of logic to practical reasoning problems that people face in their everyday lives. Technical terminology is kept to a minimum and elaborate artificial systemization is avoided.

The title, *Ordinary Logic*, derives from two facts: (1) that the concern is with the reasoning problems of people in their everyday lives, whether they be philosophers doing philosophy, mechanics, Supreme Court Justices, pilots, or housewives; and (2) that the ordinary meaning of basic logical terms is preserved in this book. You are not asked to learn new artificial meanings for terms with which you are already quite familiar.

However, if you are a student seeking an academic major in philosophy, you will not find the logic coverage in this book sufficient for your purposes, not because the philosophical reasoning you will do requires more apparatus, but rather because many of the problems in contemporary philosophy arise out of, or are often put in terms of, the conceptual apparatus of modern symbolic logic. A student with an academic major in philosophy should regard this book as an introduction to some basic ideas and strategies which will require supplementation elsewhere.

This book can serve as a self-teaching device, because of the frequent exercises to which answers are provided in the back of the book. Intelligent use of this combination of exercises and answers calls for a person who is working through the book on his own to do at least the first two and last two exercises of even the simplest-appearing exercise sets, checking his answers with those provided. Any discrepancies should either be explained, or eliminated by restudy. If restudy is called for, then presumably all the exercises in a set should be done and checked. In any case the doing of exercises is absolutely essential for learning logic, whether on your own or under supervision of an instructor. Explanations and principles which seem obvious when presented have a habit of being more difficult when applied.

The book is organized so that certain more advanced sections (labeled '∴') can be omitted without destroying continuity. I do not recommend their omission, but have provided this means for a person in a hurry to pick up some basic logic ideas. I definitely recommend against the omission of Chapter 5, "Practical Applications of Deductive Logic", because even a little logic is not of use unless it can be applied.

You will probably find that things start easy and get more difficult. But if you have trouble with the early parts not labeled '∴', I urge you to work very hard at them; for understanding them is either a prerequisite for what comes later or is essential for a basic grasp of logic.

CHAPTER 2

Basic Ideas

This book first attempts to present a simple account of common forms of deductive reasoning by describing these forms and suggesting ways of judging whether the reasoning is satisfactory. We will not consider other types of reasoning, except as contrasts to deductive reasoning. But one should remember that there are other types of reasoning, and that the ways of judging deductive reasoning do not directly apply to these other types.

DEDUCTIVE REASONING is that sort of reasoning in which the conclusion is supposed to follow necessarily from what is given. It is this fact that distinguishes deductive reasoning from all other types of reasoning. If the conclusion is supposed to follow necessarily, then we apply the standards of deductive reasoning.

Should you be in doubt about the meaning of 'follows necessarily', then the following might help—if your doubt is an unsophisticated one. If, on the other hand, your doubt is a sophisticated one, then the following interpretation will not help; for purposes of your study of this book, you already understand well enough the concept, *necessarily follows*. Here is the interpretation:

> To say "A conclusion FOLLOWS NECESSARILY from what is given" is to say: "If you accept what is given, you are thereby automatically committed to accepting the conclusion; there is no way out." It is also to say: "You would be contradicting yourself to accept what is given and deny the conclusion."

Now to say that a conclusion follows necessarily does not mean that you **do** accept what is given, nor that you **do** accept this conclusion. It merely means that **IF** you accept what is given, you are committed inescapably to the conclusion.

Some Basic Terms

In order to make it easier to talk about deductive reasoning, we will use certain basic terms with which you may already be familiar, but which are somtimes confusing if not explained. These terms are 'premise', 'argument', and 'validity'.

The PREMISES are what is given. An ARGUMENT is a set of one or more premises and a conclusion such that the conclusion is supposed to follow from the premises. Here is an argument which contains two premises and a conclusion: the solid line separates the premises from the conclusion. The premises are above the line and the conclusion below.

Example 2-1
If Mike is a dog, then Mike is an animal.
Mike is a dog.

Mike is an animal.

The argument consists of all three statements. The premises (or what is given) are the first two statements, and the conclusion is the last one.

The word 'VALID' will here be used to apply to arguments in which the conclusion follows necessarily from the premises and the word 'INVALID' for those in which the conclusion does **not** necessarily follow. This is standard usage in the field of logic. However, there is a danger in this usage; often, perfectly good arguments (which are thus valid in the ordinary sense of 'valid') are invalid in our technical sense. Unfortunately some people have the inclination, after judging such an argument invalid in this technical sense, to then claim that the argument is invalid in the ordinary sense of the term 'invalid', which is to say that the argument is defective. Many arguments are invalid in this technical sense but ought to be judged by criteria other than those for deductive arguments.

If we apply the criteria for validity (in the technical sense) to such arguments, declare the argument invalid, and then interpret our declaration according to the ordinary sense of 'invalid', we find ourselves rejecting good arguments. In our technical sense of 'valid', most cases of reasoning to generalizations in science are invalid, because the conclusions do not follow necessarily from the evidence. But we must not thereby conclude that such reasoning is defective. It just is not deductive reasoning. So please keep in mind the fact that 'valid' is being used in a technical sense in deductive logic, and that the standards of validity that you will learn do not apply to non-deductive arguments.*

Truth and Validity

In this technical sense of 'validity', judgments about the truth of a conclusion are quite distinct from judgments about the validity of the argument. A valid argument can have a false conclusion and one or more false premises. Here is an example:

Example 2-2
If the piece of iron is in the beaker containing water, then it is floating on the water.
The piece of iron is in the beaker containing water.

It is floating on the water.

The first premise is false; the conclusion is false; but the argument **is valid**, because the conclusion follows necessarily from the premises.

Of course a valid argument can have true premises and a true conclusion. For example:

Example 2-3
If the piece of iron is in the beaker of water, it is at the bottom.
The piece of iron is in the beaker of water.

It is at the bottom.

Again the conclusion follows necessarily from the premises.

Perhaps you do not realize that an argument can be valid and the conclusions can be true, even though one or more of the premises are false. Here is an illustration:

Example 2-4
Bananas are magnets.
Magnets are fruit.

Bananas are fruit.

The argument is valid; both premises are false, but the conclusion is true. The moral to be learned from the preceding example is this: the fact that

---

* Valuable discussions of this point may be found in F. L. Will's "Generalization and Evidence," an essay in Max Black's *Philosophical Analysis* (Ithaca, N.Y.: Cornell University Press, 1950), pp. 384–413; and in J. O. Urmson's "Some Questions Concerning Validity," an essay in Antony Flew's *Essays in Conceptual Analysis* (London: Macmillan & Co. Ltd., 1956), pp. 120–133.

a premise is false, even though the argument be valid, does not by itself prove that the conclusion is false.

But if the premises are true and the argument is valid, then the conclusion must be true. It is this fact that we often exploit when using deduction in a proof. Generally, we show or assume the premises to be true; we show the argument to be valid; and thus we show that the conclusion must be true. Another way to use this fact is to show that an argument is valid and that the conclusion is false. From this we know that at least one of the premises is false. This second procedure is called indirect proof. This fact about validity can also be used to show an argument to be invalid; if we show the premises to be true and the conclusion to be false, then we have shown the argument to be invalid; for a valid argument cannot have true premises and a false conclusion.

The above discussion of the relationship between truth and validity can be summarized in the following charts. The first chart shows the possible combinations for valid arguments:

CHART 2-1   Combinations for Valid Arguments

	True premises	One or more false premises
True conclusion	Possible	Possible
False conclusion	Not possible	Possible

The second chart shows the possible combinations for invalid arguments:

CHART 2-2   Combinations for Invalid Arguments

	True premises	One or more false premises
True conclusion	Possible	Possible
False conclusion	Possible	Possible

Thus all combinations but one are possible. The impossible combination is seen in the first chart: a valid argument having true premises cannot have a false conclusion.

Emphasis on Criteria

This is not a book on psychology and does not attempt to describe what goes on in people's minds when they reason. Instead we shall concentrate on the results of such processes, whatever they might be. When speaking of reasoning, I shall be referring to that which can be produced in words and laid out in the form of an argument, and shall not be referring to the process of producing arguments.

I shall emphasize the **criteria** (standards of judgment) to be used in evaluating arguments, rather than the **process** of reasoning. This emphasis will be dominant, even though I shall try to give you some hints about how to go about discovering conclusions that do and do not follow necessarily, and shall give hints about how to make judgments more efficiently. I am assuming that guided practice in applying the proper criteria will result in higher quality and more efficient processes of producing arguments.

Types of Deductive Reasoning

No one has ever successfully categorized all types of deductive reasoning, so I cannot give you a total picture into which the material in this book fits. But I can say that the kinds of deductive reasoning that you will encounter here are very commonly found in all walks of life.

Roughly following a fairly traditional division in the field of logic, I have divided the deductive reasoning to be considered into two types: sentence reasoning and class reasoning, so named because of the basic units involved, the sentence and the class. In sentence reasoning, the basic sentence units appear and reappear in the argument, but they do not change in meaning (although they might be rephrased for stylistic purposes). Sentences thus are the building blocks of sentence reasoning.

Example 2-1 above is sentence reasoning. Each of these sentences appears twice in the argument:

Mike is a dog.
Mike is an animal.

In their first appearance they are connected using the words 'if' and 'then' and form a more complicated sentence. In the second appearance, each stands by itself. Here again is the complete argument:

If Mike is a dog, then Mike is an animal.
Mike is a dog.
_____

Mike is an animal.

You can see that the two basic sentences are the units of that argument.

If the first premise (the 'if-then' premise) reads 'he is an animal' instead of 'Mike is an animal', this does not make any difference; the result is still sentence reasoning, even though one of the sentences is changed in wording for reasons of style:

Example 2-5
If Mike is a dog, then he is an animal.
Mike is a dog.
_____

Mike is an animal.

In that argument, we treat 'he is an animal' and 'Mike is an animal' as the same sentence, so in effect the sentences do not change in meaning throughout.

Example 2-4 above is class reasoning. It contains no sentence which appears and reappears unchanged. It instead focuses on three classes and their relationships. The classes are *bananas*, *magnets*, and *fruit*. Here again is the complete argument, which, you will remember, is valid, though the premises are both false:

Bananas are magnets.
Magnets are fruit.
_____

Bananas are fruit.

Chapter Summary

By now you should have at least a rough understanding of what a deductive argument is, and be familiar with the following terms: 'follows necessarily', 'premise', 'conclusion', 'argument', 'valid', and 'deductive reasoning'. The distinction between truth and validity should be clear to you. You should also know that if the argument is valid and the premises are true, then the conclusion must be true.

COMPREHENSION SELF-TEST

True or false? If the statement is false, change a crucial term (or terms) to make it true.

2–1. Deductive reasoning is that kind of reasoning in which the conclusion is supposed to follow necessarily from the premises.

2–2. If a conclusion follows necessarily, then it would be contradictory to deny the premises while asserting the conclusion.

2–3. To say that an argument is valid (in the ordinary sense of 'valid') is to say that the conclusion follows necessarily from the premises.

Answer the following:

2–4. What combination of truth and validity is impossible?

2–5. Define 'argument'.

CHAPTER 3

Sentence Reasoning

Conditional Reasoning

One very important kind of sentence reasoning is conditional reasoning, so named because it involves the use of conditions, which are often introduced by the word 'if'. This example, which you have seen before is conditional reasoning:

Example 3-1
If Mike is a dog, then Mike is an animal.
Mike is a dog.

Mike is an animal.

The first premise is a CONDITIONAL. It gives a condition (Mike's being a dog) which, according to that premise, would make Mike an animal. Since this reasoning makes use of a conditional, it is called CONDITIONAL REASONING.

Let us look very carefully at that first premise. Note what it tells us and what it does not tell us. Presumably you are agreed that it gives a condition (Mike's being a dog) which, according to the premise, would make Mike an animal. But it does **not** say that Mike's being an animal is a condition which would make Mike a dog. By substituting 'Mike is an animal' as the second premise,* it would not be established as the conclusion that Mike

---

* If Mike is a dog, then Mike is an animal.
Mike is an animal.

Mike is a dog.

is a dog. On the other hand, given the first premise and that Mike **is** a dog, it **would** thereby be established that Mike is an animal. The first premise enables us to go from Mike's being a dog to Mike's being an animal, but it does not enable us to go from Mike's being an animal to Mike's being a dog, because it does not say that Mike's being an animal is a **condition** which would necessarily make Mike a dog.

The antecedent and the consequent

Before we say more about what that first premise would enable us to do, two technical terms should be introduced, terms which are used to label the two sentences which make up a conditional statement. The sentence which follows the word 'if' is called the ANTECEDENT. In the above example, 'Mike is a dog' is the antecedent. The sentence which follows the word 'then' is called the CONSEQUENT. In the above example, 'Mike is an animal' is the consequent.

There are several different ways of writing the conditional statement, but the antecedent and the consequent do not change. For example, the word 'then' can often be omitted:

If Mike is a dog, Mike is an animal.

The order can be reversed (so long as the word 'if' stays with the antecedent):

Mike is an animal, if Mike is a dog.

In both examples 'Mike is a dog' is the antecedent, and 'Mike is an animal' is the consequent. Other ways of writing the conditional will be presented later when we deal with the expression 'only if'.

The four basic forms

In the language of antecedents and consequents, we can restate what was said about what that first premise enables us to do. Given a conditional statement (containing an antecedent and a consequent), establishment of the antecedent enables us to conclude the consequent; but establishment of the consequent does not thereby enable us to conclude the antecedent.

Example 3-1 then is a valid argument. It contains a conditional statement as a premise. Another premise consists of the affirmation of the antecedent. The conclusion consists of the consequent. This is a common form of valid deductive argument and is called AFFIRMING THE ANTECEDENT.

The following argument is somewhat different. Is it valid?

Example 3-2
If Mike is a dog, then Mike is an animal.
Mike is an animal.
_____

Mike is a dog.

You will remember that, given the first premise as it stands, Mike's being an animal does not force us to conclude that Mike is a dog. This argument is a case of AFFIRMING THE CONSEQUENT. It is called this because the second premise affirms the consequent of the conditional statement of the first premise. It is an invalid form of argument; for establishing the consequent does not enable us to conclude the antecedent.

So far you have seen two different arguments making use of the same conditional first premise. The first, which proceeded by way of affirmation of the antecedent, is valid. The second, which affirmed the consequent, is invalid.

Consider now this argument, which exemplifies a third form:

Example 3-3
If Mike is a dog, then Mike is an animal.
Mike is not a dog.
_____

Mike is not an animal.

This is not a valid argument for the conclusion does not necessarily follow. The first premise says that Mike's being a dog would make him an animal, but it does not say that his **not** being a dog would make him a nonanimal. He might be a fox. He thus might still be an animal, even though he is not a dog.

This third form of argument, as you might have already guessed, is called DENYING THE ANTECEDENT. It is an invalid form. Given a conditional statement, the denial of the antecedent does not by itself force us to conclude the denial of the consequent.

The following example (3-4) illustrates a fourth argument form. Many people are confused by this type of argument. As you read it over, see if you can tell intuitively whether the conclusion follows necessarily:

Example 3-4
If Mike is a dog, then Mike is an animal.
Mike is not an animal.
_____

Mike is not a dog.

In this example the second premise is the denial of the consequent of the conditional premise. This form of argument is called DENYING THE CONSEQUENT. It is a valid form. Given the denial of the consequent, the appropriate conclusion is the denial of the antecedent. When faced with such arguments, some people do not immediately see that they are valid—that is, that the conclusion does necessarily follow. If you are such a person, then read this next passage carefully.

The first premise tells us that Mike's being a dog would make him an animal. But, if he is not an animal, then he could not possibly be a dog, because **if** he were a dog, then he **would** be an animal. Since the second premise tells us that he is not an animal, we are forced to conclude that he is not a dog. Thus the argument is valid.

If the explanation in the preceding paragraph does not satisfy you, then make up some simple examples of your own. These examples should consist of a conditional statement and a denial of its consequent. After thinking about these examples, you will see that you are forced by the denial of the consequent to deny the antecedent also. Keep thinking about them until you do see this.

Here is a chart which summarizes what has been said about the four basic forms of conditional reasoning. See that you **understand** and not merely memorize it.

CHART 3-1   Validity of the Four Basic Forms of Conditional Reasoning

	Antecedent	Consequent
Affirming	Valid	Invalid
Denying	Invalid	Valid

In summary, affirming the antecedent and denying the consequent are valid forms of argument. That is, an appropriate conclusion **follows necessarily** when the antecedent is affirmed, or when the consequent is denied. On the other hand, affirming the consequent and denying the antecedent are invalid forms.

COMPREHENSION SELF-TEST

For each of the following conditionals, decide which part is the antecedent and which is the consequent. Indicate this by underlining the antecedent once and the consequent twice. Do not allow your underlining to extend to the logical connectives, 'if' and 'then'. The first one is a sample.

3-1. If Mike is a dog, then Mike is an animal.

3-2. Mike is an animal, if Mike is a dog.

3-3. If Mary knows the rules of punctuation, then she did well on the test today.

3-4. If John is nearsighted, his eyes are defective.

3–5. John's eyes are defective, if he is nearsighted.

3–6. If in that sentence the word 'going' is a gerund, then it functions like a noun.

3–7. Mike, if he is a dog, is an animal.

3–8. The soil in your field is sweet, if Jones added the truckload of calcium carbonate to it.

3–9. If the President is not going to veto this bill, the Senate will not stand by him in his efforts to get his tax legislation passed.

3–10. Angles A and B, if they are alternate interior angles of parallel lines, are equal.

3–11. Joan's room has light-colored walls, if it is well lighted.

3–12. If the music room does not have light-colored walls, then it is not well lighted.

3–13. The livingroom, if Mrs. Smith likes it, is well lighted.

Here is a set of arguments. With each argument do two things. State the form of the argument and tell whether the argument is valid or invalid. The first is a sample. Remember that the premises are the sentences above the line, the conclusion the sentence below the line.

3–14. If Mary knows the rules of punctuation, then she did well on the test today. Mary did not do well on the test today.

Mary does not know the rules of punctuation.
(Answer: Denying the Consequent. Valid.)

3–15. If John is nearsighted, then his eyes are defective. His eyes are defective.

John is nearsighted.

3–16. John's eyes are defective, if he is nearsighted. John is nearsighted.

John's eyes are defective.

3–17. If in that sentence the word 'going' is a gerund, then it functions like a noun. It does not function like a noun (in that sentence).

In that sentence the word 'going' is not a gerund.

3–18. The soil in your field is sweet, if Jones added the truckload of calcium carbonate to it.
The soil in your field is sweet.

He added that truckload of calcium carbonate.

3–19. If the President is not going to veto this bill, then the Senate will not stand by him in his efforts to get his tax legislation passed.
The President is not going to veto this bill.

The Senate will not stand by him in his efforts to get his tax legislation passed.

3–20. Angles A and B, if they are alternate interior angles of parallel lines, are equal. Angles A and B are not alternate interior angles of parallel lines.

They are not equal.

In this next set of problems you will be given two premises and you will be asked to supply the valid conclusion, if any. More specifically, do these two things:

a. If there is a valid conclusion other than the repetition of one of the premises, supply it. Otherwise write 'Nothing follows necessarily'.

b. State the form involved. You might well abbreviate.

Avoid doing these exercises mechanically. Make sure that you see and feel the answers that you give. The first two are samples.

3–21. Premises:

Joan's room has light-colored walls, if it is well lighted.

Joan's room is well lighted.

(Answer: Joan's room has light-colored walls. Affirming the antecedent.)

3–22. Premises:

If the sewing room is not well lighted, then it has dark-colored walls.

The sewing room is well lighted.

(Answer: Nothing necessarily follows. Denying the antecedent.)

3–23. Premises:

If the sewing room is well lighted, then it has light-colored walls.

The sewing room is well lighted.

3–24. Premises:

If the sewing room has light-colored walls, then it is well lighted.

The sewing room is not well lighted.

3–25. Premises:

The kitchen is not well lighted, if it has dark-colored walls.

The kitchen has dark-colored walls.

3–26. Premises:

If my new office has dark-colored walls, then it is not well lighted.

It is well lighted.

3–27. Premises:

If the music room does not have light-colored walls, then it is not well lighted.

The music room is well lighted.

3–28. Premises: (There are two forms combined here. Identify each. For your conclusion, make use of all of the premises.)

If the livingroom has dark-colored walls, then it is not well lighted.

The livingroom is well lighted, if Mrs. Smith likes it.

Mrs. Smith likes the livingroom.

Order of premises

Although the examples so far considered have presented the conditional statement as the first premise, the order of the premises can be changed without affecting the logical status of the argument. And you will remember that the order of the parts in the conditional statement can be changed, as long as the word 'if' remains attached to the same part. So the following example is logically the same as Example 3-1, even though the conditional statement appears second, and even though the antecedent of the conditional statement is the second half of that statement. Example 3-5 is thus in the valid form, affirming the antecedent:

Example 3-5
Mike is a dog.
Mike is an animal, if Mike is a dog.

Mike is an animal.

The converse

One change in particular is not automatically permissable, namely the **exchange** of the antecedent and consequent in a conditional statement. For instance, the following two conditional statements are different in meaning and you do not have the right to substitute one for the other:

If Mike is a dog, then Mike is an animal.
If Mike is an animal, then Mike is a dog.

The first says that Mike's being a dog would enable you to conclude that he is an animal, but it does **not** say that his being an animal would enable you to conclude that he is a dog. This last is just what the second sentence says, so the two are different in meaning.

These two sentences are called CONVERSES of each other. The converse of a conditional statement is the same statement with the antecedent and consequent exchanged. An important rule to remember, which should be obvious from an inspection of these two converses, is that the converse does not follow necessarily from a conditional statement.

The contrapositive

Consider this pair of conditionals:

If Mike is a dog, then Mike is an animal.
If Mike is not an animal, then Mike is not a dog.

Do they say the same thing? For our purposes in deductive logic, they do, but this is sometimes difficult to see.

Suppose we know that the first conditional is true. That is, suppose we know that if Mike is a dog, then he is an animal. From this we can tell that if he is not an animal, then he is not a dog. (The denial of the consequent requires the denial of the antecedent.) So the second conditional follows necessarily from the first.

Does the first follow necessarily from the second? Suppose we know that if Mike is not an animal, then Mike is not a dog. Suppose we also know that Mike is a dog. Then he would have to be an animal, for if he were not, then he would not be a dog. Thus from the second conditional the first also follows necessarily.

Since each of these follows necessarily from the other, for our purposes, they can be treated as meaning the same thing. We can substitute each for the other as a proper step in an argument.

In terms of antecedents and consequents, you should note that each of these can be formed by exchanging and denying the antecedent and consequent of the other. The antecedent of the second conditional is the denial of the consequent of the first, and the consequent of the second conditional is the denial of the antecedent of the first. Going the other way (from the second to the first) involves the principle of double negation, so a word about it is in order.

Double negation

The principle of double negation is this: Two negatives make a positive. (Actually you have already used this principle in doing Exercise 3-27.) Although there are difficulties with it, for purposes of elementary logic this principle is a good one. If you were to say that Mike is **not** a dog and someone else were to say, "That's false", then he in effect would be saying that Mike **is** a dog. His denial of your negative statement amounts to the positive statement, "Mike is a dog."

So a denial of the consequent of the second of the above pair of contrapositives amounts to the antecedent of the first of the pair. Similarly the denial of the antecedent of the second of the pair is the consequent of the first. So you can see that a contrapositive can be formed by denying and exchanging the antecedent and consequent of a conditional statement. Since contrapositives are essentially equivalent in meaning, this formation of contrapositives can be useful in deductive proofs, because they can be substituted for each other. This application of the principle of double negation to the formation of contrapositives is but one of its many uses.

COMPREHENSION SELF-TEST

True or false? If the statement is false, change a crucial term (or terms) to make it true.

3–29. A conditional statement is equivalent to its converse.

3–30. A conditional statement is equivalent to its contrapositive.

3–31. For purposes of elementary logic, two negatives make a positive.

3–32. For purposes of elementary logic the order of the premises with respect to each other sometimes affects the validity of the argument.

Short-answer Questions. **3–33** through **3–45.** Take each of the conditionals listed in 3–1 through 3–13 and write out the converse and contrapositive of each. As an example, 3–33 is done below:

SAMPLE: 3–33

a. Converse: If Mike is an animal, then Mike is a dog.

b. Contrapositive. If Mike is not an animal, then Mike is not a dog.

Here is a set of arguments. In each case judge the validity of the argument and indicate your reason. The first two are samples. Some of them serve to review earlier sections.

3–46. If the majority leader is against the bill, then Senator Jones is against it.

If Senator Jones is not against the bill, then the majority leader is not against it. (Answer: Valid. Contraposition.)

3–47. Senator Jones is against the bill, if the majority leader is against it.

If Senator Jones is against the bill, then the majority leader is against it. (Answer: Invalid. Conversion.)

3–48. If Senator Jones is against the bill, then the Commissioner testified vigorously in its favor.
It is false that Senator Jones is not against the bill.

The Commissioner testified vigorously in its favor.

3–49. If the object of the preposition is written correctly, then it is in the objective case.
The object of that preposition is in the objective case.

The object of that preposition is written correctly.

3–50. Emilia thinks Iago to be essentially good throughout most of *Othello*.
If Iago is really supposed to be a melodramatic villain, then Emilia would not think Iago to be essentially good throughout the play.

Iago is not really supposed to be a melodramatic villain.

3–51. The question mark is not inside the quotation marks.
The quoted material is not a question, if the question mark is not inside the quotation marks.

The quoted material is not a question.

3–52. There is no dot between the two numbers.

Those two numbers should be multiplied together, if there is a dot between them.

The numbers should not be multiplied together.

3–53. If the litmus did not turn red, then the liquid is not an acid.

If the liquid is an acid, the litmus turned red.

3–54. If there are no leaves on the tree, then it is dead.

If the tree is dead, then there are no leaves on it.

3–55. If the power was not increased, the plane did not gain altitude.

If the plane gained altitude, the power was increased.

3–56. Smith cannot lift the elephant, if the mechanical advantage is not over thirty.

If the mechanical advantage is over thirty, then Smith can lift the elephant.

Putting an argument in shape

Unfortunately, arguments that we meet while doing the work of the world do not come served up to us in the tidy form of those you have been considering. Here is an example of something that is in a form that you might meet:

Example 3-6

I am convinced that the lighting in the livingroom is satisfactory. There can be no doubt about this, for it follows from the following reasons: If the lighting in the livingroom is indirect, then Mrs. Smith will like it. And one thing is clear— Mrs. Smith is a fair judge. If she does not like it, then it is clearly unsatisfactory. This morning she said that the lighting in the livingroom is indirect. My conclusion is therefore obvious.

The above argument, when taken as a whole, is fairly complicated. Let us rearrange it so it is in a more workable form. The first thing to do is to locate the conclusion. In this case the conclusion is **indicated** by the first sentence, but it is not exactly the first sentence; for the speaker is not trying to prove that he is convinced of something, but rather that the thing of which he is convinced is so. What is the thing of which he is convinced? The following:

The lighting in the livingroom is satisfactory.

When the argument is put in form, this sentence, the conclusion, will appear last. We can leave the next sentence ("There can be no doubt about this, for it follows from the following reasons:") out of the completed argument.

This sentence merely shows that the first sentence is the conclusion and that the reasons (premises) come next. It does not contribute to the content of the argument.

The third sentence provides us with one of the premises. It is the first one to write down:

If the lighting in the livingroom is indirect, then Mrs. Smith will like it.

The fourth sentence, which claims that Mrs. Smith is a fair judge, does not in this case play a clear role in the argument, although it adds to the flavor and might be treated as a vague statement of the next premise, which appears as the following sentence, the fifth:

If she does not like it, then it is clearly unsatisfactory.

To return to the fourth sentence, a question might be raised about whether it implies the converse of the fifth sentence. That is, someone might suggest that it implies the following:

If it is clearly unsatisfactory, then she will not like it.

This is a difficult but important matter to settle, because (to look ahead) adopting this interpretation of the fourth sentence will make the argument valid; the argument is invalid if we reject this converse as a legitimate interpretation. Must it be that a **fair** judge will not like unsatisfactory things? If you say yes, then you are committed to the converse as an interpretation.

The important thing to see here is that there is sometimes a choice to be made in the interpretation of the premises, and that the validity of an argument sometimes depends upon the decision. In this particular case I shall proceed as if this converse interpretation is incorrect, because I believe that fair judges can correctly judge things unsatisfactory, even if such judges do personally like the unsatisfactory things. Mrs. Smith, though a fair judge, might personally like the lighting in the livingroom, although by the accepted standards of lighting, she might properly judge it unsatisfactory. But this is a point that might be argued against by reasonable men, so a legitimate problem of interpretation exists.

In solving such problems of interpretation, one usually does well to err on the side of caution. Then you can say to the person offering the argument something like the following:

Look, the conclusion does not follow necessarily if we interpret the premises strictly. Would you care to add this explicitly as a premise: "If it is unsatisfactory, then she will not like it"? If not, then the conclusion does not follow necessarily. If so, then you must be confident of the truth of this additional premise, and be able to back it up.

Having been cautious in the interpretation, you can force a person to choose between having: (1) an invalid argument, and (2) another premise that he must be able to defend.

The sixth sentence in the original argument gives us the third premise, although again we must make an adjustment, because the statement holds only that she **said** that the lighting was indirect, rather than explicitly stating, "the lighting in the livingroom is indirect." So we must adjust the premise (on the assumption that what she said is true) and write it as follows:

The lighting in the livingroom is indirect.

Again there is room for dispute about whether to adjust that sentence. In this case we will proceed as if this is a legitimate adjustment, but we do want to note the possibility of error of interpretation.

Given the above interpretations let us rewrite the argument in better form:

Example 3-7
If the lighting in the livingroom is indirect, then Mrs. Smith will like it.
If she does not like it, then it is clearly unsatisfactory.
The lighting in the livingroom is indirect.

The lighting in the livingroom is satisfactory.

Now what do you do? You inspect the premises to see if there is a valid way of going to the conclusion. Inspection shows that the first and third premises can be taken as a separate argument which will yield a subconclusion that is related to the first premise. This subargument is valid because the antecedent is affirmed. It looks as follows:

Example 3-8
If the lighting in the livingroom is indirect, then Mrs. Smith will like it.
The lighting in the livingroom is indirect.

Mrs. Smith will like it.

Does this subconclusion help in arriving at a valid argument yielding the main conclusion? Let us combine this subconclusion with the original second premise in a separate argument:

Example 3-9
If she does not like it, then it is clearly unsatisfactory.
She will like it (or she does like it).

It is satisfactory.

This second subargument (Example 3-9) is invalid because it makes use of the denial of the antecedent.

An inspection of the three premises shows that there is no other plausible way to combine the three premises, so we must judge the entire argument invalid. If one part of a complex argument is invalid, then the entire argument is invalid, since the conclusion does not follow necessarily from the premises.

In this section on putting an argument into shape, you have seen that the conclusion might very well not appear at the end of the argument; that the premises might not be in the most convenient order; that there is sometimes material that is not part of the substance of the argument; that decisions must often be made about the interpretation of the premises; and that these decisions should be made conservatively. The order in which to do these things is roughly that in which they were done for the example, but do not follow this advice rigidly. Sometimes a decision on an earlier step (for example, what the conclusion really is) might be affected by a decision on a later step (for example, the validity of the argument). We might decide that a particular person could not have been foolish enough to make the simple mistake about validity that we would have to attribute to him if the originally selected conclusion were the one he actually intended. So we might change our decision about what the conclusion of the argument really is on the basis of a judgment about validity.

Using symbols to represent sentences

Often it is convenient to use an arrow to represent the if-then relationship and to use single letters to stand for the sentences of sentence reasoning. The letters, 'p', 'q', 'r', etc., are conventional symbols.

Let 'p' stand for 'Mike is a dog', and let 'q' stand for 'Mike is an animal'. Then the conditional, 'If Mike is a dog, then Mike is an animal', can be represented as follows:

$$p \longrightarrow q$$

Note that this is quite different from the converse, 'If Mike is an animal, then Mike is a dog', which would be represented this way (assuming the same assignment of letters):

$$q \longrightarrow p$$

Thus '$q \longrightarrow p$' does not necessarily follow from '$p \longrightarrow q$'; and, of course, '$p \longrightarrow q$' does not necessarily follow from '$q \longrightarrow p$'.

The contrapositive of the original, 'If Mike is not an animal, then Mike is not a dog', would be symbolized as follows (assuming the same assignment of letters):

$$\text{not } q \longrightarrow \text{not } p$$

The conditional, 'not $q \longrightarrow$ not p', follows necessarily from '$p \longrightarrow q$', and vice versa, since contrapositives follow necessarily from each other. But be careful, because 'not $p \rightarrow$ not q' does not necessarily follow from '$p \rightarrow q$'; or, in other words, the falsity of the antecedent does not imply the falsity of the consequent. This fact is another way of stating the principle that denial of the antecedent is an invalid form.

In symbolized form the antecedent always appears first and the arrow always points to the right. This is so even if the antecedent appears last in the premise as written. Remember that the following two statements are the same:

> If Mike is a dog, then Mike is an animal.
> Mike is an animal, if Mike is a dog.

Assuming the previous assignment of letters, each of these two statements would be symbolized as follows:

$$p \rightarrow q$$

They have the same antecedent and the same consequent. The order of appearance is antecedent, arrow, and consequent.

Let us consider the simple argument of Example 3-1 in order to see the procedures to follow in symbolizing an argument and judging its validity. That argument looked like this:

> If Mike is a dog, then Mike is an animal.
> Mike is a dog.
> _____
> Mike is an animal.

The first thing to do is to assign the letters, making sure that no one letter is assigned to two different sentences, unless they differ only by virtue of the fact that one is the negation of the other, in which case you would assign the same letter. (If, for example, you had assigned the letter 'p' to represent the sentence 'Mike is a dog', then 'Mike is not a dog' would be symbolized as 'not p'.) Make sure that no extra letters are unnecessarily assigned. Write out your assignment of symbols to represent the different sentences in the argument:

> Let 'p' = 'Mike is a dog'
> Let 'q' = 'Mike is an animal'

Sometimes you can save time (but you must be careful) by simply writing the letters over the first appearance of each sentence involved, as shown here:

$$\underbrace{p}_{\text{If Mike is a dog, then}} \quad \underbrace{q}_{\text{Mike is an animal.}}$$

The next step is to write out the entire argument in symbolic form, as follows:

Example 3-10
Premises:
$$p \longrightarrow q$$
$$p$$
Conclusion:
$$q$$

You should recognize that form as the valid form, **affirmation of the antecedent**.

Symbolization of the other three basic forms looks as follows:

Affirming the consequent	Denying the antecedent	Denying the consequent
$p \longrightarrow q$	$p \longrightarrow q$	$p \longrightarrow q$
q	not p	not q
---	---	---
p	not q	not p
(An invalid form)	(An invalid form)	(A valid form)

The argument that was discussed in the previous section, "Putting an Argument in Shape", would be symbolized as follows:

Example 3-11
Let 'p' = 'the lighting in the livingroom is indirect'
Let 'q' = 'Mrs. Smith will like it'
Let 'r' = 'the lighting in the livingroom is unsatisfactory'

$$p \longrightarrow q$$
$$\text{not } q \longrightarrow r$$
$$p$$
$$\overline{\text{not } r}$$

An inspection of the symbolized argument shows that the third premise affirms the antecedent of the first premise, validly producing 'q'. But 'q' is the denial of the antecedent of the second premise, so the move to a denial of the consequent of the second premise, if that move is based upon 'q', is not a valid move.

Thinking of the argument as having two stages may be clearer. The first yields an intermediate conclusion:

Stage 1.
$$p \longrightarrow q$$
$$p$$
$$\overline{q}$$
Valid. Affirming the Antecedent.

In the second stage the intermediate conclusion ('q') is used as one of the premises:

Stage 2.
  not $q \longrightarrow r$
  q
  _____
  not r
Invalid. Denial of the Antecedent.

So the whole argument is judged invalid.

The reason for introducing the use of symbols should now be apparent to you. Symbols make the basic structure of arguments easier to see. With practice, a glance at the premises of a symbolized argument will reveal its validity or invalidity.

COMPREHENSION SELF-TEST

True or false? If the statement is false, change a crucial term (or terms) to make it true.

3–57. The order in which the premises appear does not affect the validity of the argument.

3–58. The last sentence of an argument in its natural state is always the conclusion.

3–59. An arrow pointing to the right is used to symbolize the conditional relationship.

3–60. '$q \longrightarrow p$' does not necessarily follow from '$p \longrightarrow q$'.

3–61. '$q \longrightarrow p$' does not necessarily follow from 'not $p \longrightarrow$ not q'.

Arguments to Judge. Here is a set of arguments. On a separate sheet of paper, symbolize them and put them in shape; then judge whether each is valid, explaining why you judge as you do. The first is done as a sample:

3–62. The two numbers obviously should not be multiplied together. Think of it this way. You realize that the two numbers should be multiplied together, if there is a dot between them. But there is no dot between those two numbers. So they should not be multiplied together.
Let 'p' = 'there is a dot between the two numbers'
Let 'q' = 'the two numbers should be multiplied together'
  $p \longrightarrow q$
  not p
  _____
  not q
(Answer: The argument is invalid because the antecedent is denied.)

3–63. Jones must be at least thirty-five years of age. I know this because he is President; and if he is President, then he must be at least thirty-five years of age.

3–64. If this figure is an equilateral triangle, then it has all sides equal. I conclude that it cannot be an equilateral triangle, since not all sides are equal.

3–65. If these two plants are not closely related, then they cannot be crossed. However, they are closely related. Therefore they can be crossed.

3–66. No photosynthesis can be occurring in this plant. That this is so can be seen from the fact that it is not getting any light whatsoever. Photosynthesis cannot occur in this plant, if there is no light reaching it.

3–67. "Macbeth shall never vanquished be until
Great Birnam wood to high Dunsinane hill
Shall come against him."
"That will never be."
(You must state the conclusion yourself.)

3–68. You may fly now, because the beacon is not lit. If it were lit, then you would not be permitted to fly.

3–69. I know that Senator Franklin will oppose the tax legislation. Furthermore if he opposes it, then Senator Inkling will vote in favor of it. Senator Inkling and Senator Franklin do not get along well together. If Senator Inkling votes in favor of that legislation, my wife, a loyal member of the League of Women Voters, will be busy all next year trying to get her friends and acquaintances to help defeat him at the polls. And if she and her friends are occupied with the League all next year, we won't be eating very good dinners around here for a while. That figures, doesn't it? So now you know why I expect dinners that are less than the best next year.

3–70. If the Board of Education suspends young Brown from school, then it will be punishing him for refusing to salute the flag on religious grounds. And if it does that, it will be acting unconstitutionally. Since the Board will not act unconstitutionally, we can be sure that the Board will not suspend young Brown.

Argument Forms. Using '*p*' to represent the antecedent and '*q*' to represent the consequent, fill in the gaps in the following representation of the **four** basic forms of conditional argument:

The following argument form is an example of Affirming the . . . . (**3–71**)
    Premises:
        . . . . (**3–72**)
        p
    Conclusion:
        . . . . (**3–73**)
    Is the above a valid or invalid form? (**3–74**)

The following argument form is an example of Denying the . . . . (**3–75**)
    Premises:
        $p \longrightarrow q$
        . . . . (**3–76**)
    Conclusion:

.... (**3-77**)

The above is a valid form.

The following argument is an example of .... (**3-78**) the .... (**3-79**)

Premises:

$p \longrightarrow q$

q

Conclusion:

.... (**3-80**)

Is the above a valid or invalid form? (**3-81**)

The following argument is an example of .... (**3-82**) the .... (**3-83**)

Premises:

$p \longrightarrow q$

.... (**3-84**)

Conclusion:

.... (**3-85**)

Is the above a valid or invalid form? (**3-86**)

Necessary and/or sufficient conditions

You might find, as many do, that it is often convenient, when thinking about an argument, to think in terms of necessary and/or sufficient conditions. Consider the basic example:

If Mike is a dog, then Mike is an animal.

The proposition that Mike is a dog is claimed by this statement to be a sufficient condition for the truth of the proposition that Mike is an animal. In other words, Mike's being a dog is claimed to be a sufficient condition for Mike's being an animal. If we know that Mike is a dog, then, according to that conditional, we have sufficient evidence to justify saying that he is an animal.

On the other hand, his being a dog is not held by the conditional statement to be a necessary condition for his being an animal. The statement allows that he be a fox. Thus he might be an animal without being a dog. Thus being a dog is not held to be a necessary condition for his being an animal.

But his being an animal **is** held to be a necessary condition for his being a dog. He cannot be a dog without being an animal as well, according to the statement. The truth of the proposition that Mike is an animal is held to be a necessary condition for the truth of the proposition that he is a dog.

And, of course, his being an animal is not held to be a sufficient condition for his being a dog. It is only held to be a necessary condition.

Summarizing symbolically, given $p \longrightarrow q$, the truth of p is a sufficient, but not necessary, condition for the truth of q; and the truth of q is a necessary, but not sufficient, condition for the truth of p. If the truth of one statement is a sufficient condition for the truth of another, then the truth of the other is a necessary condition for the truth of the first, and vice versa.

Let us apply the language of necessary and sufficient conditions to one of the recent exercises, 3-64:

> If this figure is an equilateral triangle, then it has all sides equal. I conclude that it cannot be an equilateral triangle, since not all sides are equal.

> Let 'p' be 'this figure is an equilateral triangle'
> Let 'q' be 'it has all sides equal'

Symbolically the argument looks like this:

Example 3-12

$p \longrightarrow q$

not q

not p (valid; denying the consequent)

One might talk about the valid argument of the above example in the following manner:

> Having all sides equal is given as a necessary condition for the figure's being an equilateral triangle. Since that necessary condition does not hold, it is not an equilateral triangle.

Symbolically, the talk might go like this:

> q is a necessary condition for p. q is false. Hence p is false.

The language of necessary and sufficient conditions is an aid to quick insight into logical arguments, because of the conceptual economy that it effects. Look again at Exercise 3-69, which is reproduced below:

> I know that Senator Franklin will oppose the tax legislation. Furthermore if he opposes it, then Senator Inkling will vote in favor of it. Senator Inkling and Senator Franklin do not get along well together. If Senator Inkling votes in favor of that legislation, my wife, a loyal member of the League of Women Voters, will be busy all next year trying to get her friends and acquaintances to help defeat him at the polls. And if she and her friends are occupied with the League all next year, we won't be eating very good dinners around here for a while. That figures, doesn't it? So now you know why I expect dinners that are less than the best next year.

Thinking about this example in the language of necessary and sufficient conditions, one might come up with the following brief analysis, which is correct:

Each condition given is a sufficient condition for the next. Since the first condition is affirmed (this occurs in the first sentence), each succeeding condition follows necessarily. Hence the conclusion, "Dinners will not be very good around here for a while", follows necessarily.

Although the use of the language of necessary and sufficient conditions is an aid to quick insight into the structure of an argument, two precautions should be noted: (1) the lack of precision of the language as often used, and (2) the distinction between the necessary and sufficient conditions of sentence reasoning and the necessary and sufficient conditions of causal relationships. For our purposes the second precaution is more important than the first, but we shall take them in order.

1. Note that a strict substitution into the statement, "q is a necessary condition for p" (one of the symbolic statements made earlier), does not make sense:

This figure has all sides equal is a necessary condition for this figure is an equilateral triangle.

In order to be precise there are basically two alternatives: (a) incorporate the sentences into broader units, as in the following example:

That this figure has all sides equal is a necessary condition for the truth of the proposition, 'This figure is an equilateral triangle'.

(b) alternatively and less awkwardly, use gerunds instead of sentences to indicate the conditions:

Having all sides equal is a necessary condition for this figure's being an equilateral triangle.

The use of gerunds, however, results in the new problem of transition from one manner of speaking to the other, a problem that matters in rigorous treatments of logic.

The standards of rigor alluded to here can generally be ignored when the language of necessary and sufficient conditions is used as an aid to insight. If, however, one wants to state a rigorous proof using this language, of course the standards cannot be ignored. .

2. The second precaution deals with the distinction between causal language and general necessary and sufficient condition language. CAUSALLY NECESSARY AND SUFFICIENT CONDITIONS are events (or states of being) such that, respectively, another event (or state of being) cannot occur without the condition, and another event (or state of being) must occur if the condition occurs.

Here is an expression of a causally necessary condition:

The presence of oxygen was a necessary condition for the burning of the building.

Here is an expression of a causally sufficient condition:

Knocking out that block of wood was a sufficient condition for the collapse of the building.

Causally necessary and sufficient conditions can often be expressed in 'if-then' language:

If the building burned, then oxygen was present.
If that block of wood was knocked out, then the building collapsed.

The point is that causally necessary and sufficient conditions are only one kind of necessary and sufficient conditions. Each type of such conditions requires a different kind of proof for its establishment and is applied in its own special ways. Hence it is important to know with which kind one is dealing.

Speaking of causally necessary and sufficient conditions makes sense only when the thing mentioned as a condition precedes or accompanies the thing for which it is a condition. Hence, if you tried to locate a necessary condition in the above example, "If that block of wood was knocked out, then the building collapsed", you probably had difficulty. It would seem odd to say that the collapse of the building was a necessary condition for the knocking out of the block of wood, as that would imply that the collapse of the building preceded the knocking out of the block of wood, since we are dealing with a causal relationship.

However, the truth of the statement that the building collapsed is a necessary condition for the truth of the statement that the block of wood was knocked out, according to the original conditional. For if the building did not collapse, then according to the original, the block of wood could not have been knocked out. Thus, as long as we speak strictly in terms of sentence-reasoning necessary and sufficient conditions, 'p' in '$p \longrightarrow q$' always is a sufficient condition and 'q' always is a necessary condition. But, if we start speaking in terms of events or states of affairs, then we sometimes end up with odd results if the two items are causally connected.

Only if

So far no examples have contained the words, 'only if', because this phrase is rather different from 'if' in meaning and a danger of confusion exists. But it is time to face the problem. Consider these two statements and decide whether they mean the same:

1. Mike is a dog, only if Mike is an animal.
2. If Mike is a dog, then Mike is an animal.

As you can see, there are differences and similarities. Superficially a difference is that the word 'if' is connected with different sentences in the two statements. It is connected with 'Mike is an animal' in the first (but remember that the word 'only' is there also), whereas it is connected with 'Mike is a dog' in the second.

An important difference, so far as the use of the total statements is concerned, is that the first seems to give us a test for telling whether Mike is a dog, while the second seems to give a test for telling whether Mike is an animal. Thus we would tend to use the first in contexts in which we are trying to determine whether he is a dog, and the second in contexts in which we are trying to tell whether he is an animal.

In spite of these differences, the two statements are essentially the same for purposes of deductive logic. In each case Mike's being an animal is held to be a necessary condition for his being a dog; and his being a dog is held to be a sufficient condition for his being an animal.

Each of the statements implies the other. Suppose we know the first to be true. Then if Mike is a dog, he must be an animal; for if he is not an animal, he could not be a dog. The first does say that he is a dog **only if** he is an animal.

Working the other way, suppose we know that the second of the two statements is true. By contraposition you know from this that if Mike is not an animal, then he cannot be a dog. Or in other words he is a dog **only if** he is an animal.

Thus for our purposes the following two forms are logically equivalent:

If p, then q.
p, only if q.

Furthermore the following ones, which simply change the order, are equivalent to the above two and to each other:

q, if p.
Only if q, p.

And all of these are represented by the following elementary symbol group:

$$p \longrightarrow q$$

The definition of 'conditional' should now be extended to cover statements containing the phrase 'only if', since for our purposes such statements can be treated by the rules of conditional reasoning.

The biconditional: if, and only if

Sometimes the relationship between two sentences is such that each implies the other. For example the following two sentences imply each other:

Jones is a bachelor.
Jones is a man who is not yet married.

Since the first implies the second, we might want to say the following:

If Jones is a bachelor, then Jones is a man who is not yet married.

And we might want to say the converse, since it is also true:

If Jones is a man who is not yet married, then Jones is a bachelor.

The relationship of mutual implication can be written in one statement, a BICONDITIONAL, which makes use of the phrase, 'if, and only if':

Jones is a bachelor, if, and only if, Jones is a man who is not yet married.

The following is a longer, but logically equivalent, way to write this:

If Jones is a bachelor, then Jones is a man who is not yet married; and if Jones is a man who is not yet married, then Jones is a bachelor.

The advantage of using the phrase, 'if, and only if', should be evident; it saves time and space.

That the biconditional does state the relationship of mutual implication can be seen from the following discussion, which makes use of symbols in order to save time and space:

Let 'p' = 'Jones is a bachelor'
Let 'q' = 'Jones is a man who is not yet married'

Then we are entitled to say that if p, then q, and this entitles us to say the following:

p, only if q.

We are also entitled to say the converse, 'If q, then p'. And we are entitled

to reverse the order, leaving the 'if' with the same sentence, 'q':

p, if q.

So we have 'p, only if q' and 'p, if q'. Thus we have the biconditional:

p, if, and only if, *q*,

which means the same as:

p is a necessary and sufficient condition for *q*,

and also the same as:

q is a necessary and sufficient condition for *p*.

For convenience the biconditional is represented by a double arrow, as in the following:

$p \leftrightarrow q$

Given a biconditional, '$p \leftrightarrow q$', you are entitled to make use of either of the converse relationships between '*p*' and '*q*'. That is, you can derive each of the following from it:

$p \rightarrow q$
$q \rightarrow p$

And since each of these has a derivable contrapositive, the following can also be derived from the original biconditional:

not $q \rightarrow$ not p
not $p \rightarrow$ not q

Furthermore by an argument similar to the one that showed that '$p \rightarrow q$' and '$q \rightarrow p$' together give '$p \leftrightarrow q$', we can show that the above two contrapositives give the following biconditional:

not $p \leftrightarrow$ not q

This also follows from the original biconditional, since it follows from things that followed from the original biconditional.

In summary, given a biconditional and the affirmation of either part, the other part is implied. Furthermore, given the denial of either part, the denial of the other part is implied. Each part is a necessary and sufficient condition for the other part. Lastly, the phrase, 'if, and only if', is an accepted way of indicating the biconditional and is conveniently symbolized by a double arrow.

This treatment of biconditionals opens the door for a qualification to the earlier discussion of the rule that the antecedent does not necessarily follow from the affirmation of the consequent. Consider this argument:

Example 3-13
If Jones is a bachelor, then Jones is a man who is not yet married.
Jones is a man who is not yet married.

Jones is a bachelor.

This argument is in the invalid form, affirming the consequent. But the conclusion does follow necessarily from the premises. In fact, it follows necessarily from the second premise alone. This is so because of the definitional relationship between the second premise and the conclusion. To say that Jones is a man who is not yet married is to say that Jones is a bachelor, so each follows necessarily from the other. We have this problem whenever there is a biconditional relationship that is true by definition. Our rule can be restated, however:

> The antecedent does not necessarily follow from the affirmation of the consequent as a result of its being the consequent, although the antecedent might follow from the affirmation of the consequent for other reasons.

Similarly the rule about the denial of the antecedent might be revised to take care of a like difficulty:

> The denial of the consequent does not necessarily follow from the denial of the antecedent as a result of its being the antecedent, although the denial of the consequent might follow from the denial of the antecedent for other reasons.

These qualifications are made because people sometimes are confused by this problem. There is no point to your learning the above revised rules. Just understand them and the reason for them.

A conditional chain

Another basic form of conditional reasoning appears in the following example:

Example 3-14
If Mike barks, then Mike is a dog.
If Mike is a dog, then Mike is an animal.

If Mike barks, then Mike is an animal.

Note that in this example the conclusion itself is a conditional statement, and both premises are conditional statements. Note also that the argument is valid. One who accepts the premises is thereby committed to the conclusion. The form of the above argument can be shown as follows:

Example 3-15
Let 'p' = 'Mike barks'
Let 'q' = 'Mike is a dog'
Let 'r' = 'Mike is an animal'

$$p \longrightarrow q$$
$$q \longrightarrow r$$
$$\overline{}$$
$$p \longrightarrow r$$

This is a valid form of argument. Call it a CONDITIONAL CHAIN.

Similarly, the following is also a conditional chain, and valid argument form.

$$p \longrightarrow q$$
$$r \longrightarrow p$$
$$\overline{}$$
$$r \longrightarrow q$$

You may find it easier to recognize this as a conditional chain, if the order of the premises is reversed:

$$r \longrightarrow p$$
$$p \longrightarrow q$$
$$\overline{}$$
$$r \longrightarrow q$$

Note carefully the relationship between the parts, because there are series of conditionals that are invalid. The two conditional premises have a part in common, which serves as the antecedent of one and the consequent of the other. The remaining antecedent and consequent are put together as antecedent and consequent **respectively** of the conclusion.

Now examine these invalid arguments and see how they depart from the above criteria:

Example 3-16	**Example 3-17**	**Example 3-18**
$p \longrightarrow q$	$p \longrightarrow q$	$p \longrightarrow q$
$q \longrightarrow r$	$r \longrightarrow q$	not $q \longrightarrow r$
$r \longrightarrow p$	$p \longrightarrow r$	$p \longrightarrow r$ (or $p \longrightarrow$ not r)

In Example 3-16 the conclusion is the converse of the conclusion in Example 3-15, which is the valid argument. The trouble with Example 3-16 is that the antecedent and consequent of the conclusion do not come from the right places in the premises. Example 3-16 would be valid if its conclusion were the converse of the presented conclusion.

In example 3-17 the common part is the consequent of both premises, so even if the converse of the given conclusion had been presented the argument would still be invalid. And of course the trouble with Example 3-18 is that no common part is shared by the two premises as antecedent in one and consequent in the other. The consequent of the first premise is 'q' while the antecedent of the second premise is different. It is 'not q'. Furthermore substituting contrapositives will not solve the problem. Try it and see what happens.

Sometimes, however, it is helpful to substitute contrapositives in order to establish the form of the conditional chain. Consider this argument:

Example 3-19

If the dish of sweet and sour pork contains sufficient meat, then it is expensive. If the dish of sweet and sour pork contains several pieces of sweet pineapple, then it is not expensive.

If the dish of sweet and sour pork contains sufficient meat, then it does not contain several pieces of sweet pineapple.

First let us symbolize the argument.

Example 3-20

Let 'p' = 'the dish of sweet and sour pork contains sufficient meat'
Let 'q' = 'it is expensive'
Let 'r' = the dish of sweet and sour pork contains several pieces of sweet pineapple'

$p \longrightarrow q$
$r \longrightarrow$ not q

$p \longrightarrow$ not r

Now this argument is not in the form of the conditional chain. It could be, if the consequent of one premise were the antecedent of another. And by substituting the contrapositive of either premise, we do achieve that result. Substituting the contrapositive of the second premise ('$q \longrightarrow$ not r') for the second premise that appears ('$r \longrightarrow$ not q'), we have the following argument:

Example 3-21

$p \longrightarrow q$
$q \longrightarrow$ not r

$p \longrightarrow$ not r

Since 'q' is the consequent of the first premise and the antecedent of the next one, we can validly conclude '$p \longrightarrow$ not r', which is the conclusion of the original argument.

Instead we could have substituted the contrapositive of the first premise—with this result, also valid:

Example 3-22

not $q \longrightarrow$ not p
$r \longrightarrow$ not q

$r \longrightarrow$ not p

In this case the conclusion is the contrapositive of the original. But since we can substitute contrapositives for each other, we can substitute the original conclusion for the one that appears in Example 3-22.

Although conditional chains do not usually have many steps, they can be longer. The following is a valid argument:

Example 3-23

If the nail had not been lost, the shoe would not have been lost.
If the shoe had not been lost, the horse would not have been lost.
If the horse had not been lost, the man would not have been lost.
If the man had not been lost, the battle would not have been lost.
If the battle had not been lost, the kingdom would not have been lost.

If the nail had not been lost, the kingdom would not have been lost.

Glossing over the difference between 'had not been' and 'would not have been', symbols, assigned in the obvious way, give the following form:

Example 3-24

$p \longrightarrow q$
$q \longrightarrow r$
$r \longrightarrow s$
$s \longrightarrow t$
$t \longrightarrow v$

$p \longrightarrow v$

That this is valid can be seen by noting the following steps:

1. The first two premises give us '$p \longrightarrow r$'.
2. That result ('$p \longrightarrow r$') together with the third premise gives '$p \longrightarrow s$'.
3. That result ('$p \longrightarrow s$') together with the fourth premise gives '$p \longrightarrow t$'.
4. That result ('$p \longrightarrow t$') together with the fifth premise gives the conclusion, '$p \longrightarrow v$'.

To summarize, a basic valid form, the conditional chain, contains two conditional premises with a common part as antecedent in one and consequent in the other. The other parts of the premises form the conclusion in such a way that each of these parts preserves its original status—as antecedent or consequent. Secondly, in deciding whether an argument is equivalent to this form, it is sometimes helpful to substitute contrapositives for existing conditionals. And lastly longer conditional chains can be constructed out of the basic unit described above.

COMPREHENSION SELF-TEST

True or false? If the statement is false, change a crucial term (or terms) to make it true.

3–87. 'If p, then q' is symbolized the same way as 'p, only if q'.

3–88. 'If p, then q' is for the purposes of logic treated the same as 'p, only if q'.

3–89. 'q, if p' is symbolized in the same way as 'q, only if p'.

3–90. An arrow pointing in both directions is used to symbolize the biconditional relationship.

3–91. The following is a valid form of argument:

$$q \longrightarrow p$$
$$\underline{p }$$
$$q$$

3–92. The denial of either side of a biconditional implies the denial of the other.

3–93. A pair of conditional premises and a conditional conclusion make a valid argument, if the premises share a common antecedent.

3–94. If q is a necessary condition for p, then p is a sufficient condition for q.

3–95. Given that p is a sufficient condition for q, the falsity of q implies the falsity of p.

Arguments to Judge. Here is a set of arguments. Symbolize them and put them in shape; then judge whether each is valid, explaining why you judge as you do.

3–96. Your report is satisfactory only if every word is spelled correctly. Since your report is unsatisfactory, the obvious conclusion is that not every word is spelled correctly.

3–97. Triangles A and B are congruent, if, and only if, they have two angles and the included side equal. But they are not congruent. Therefore, they do not have two angles and the included side equal.

3–98. If the lighting in the livingroom is not indirect, then it is not satisfactory. And if it is not satisfactory, then Mrs. Smith will not like it. So, if it is not indirect, then Mrs. Smith will not like it.

3–99. If Shakespeare had intended Polonius to be a comic figure, then he would not have made Polonius the father of two tragic characters. But Polonius was made the father of two tragic characters, Laertes and Ophelia. Hence Polonius was not supposed to be a comic figure.

3–100. If Governor Jones signed the letter, then serious damage to his chances for the Vice-presidency was permitted by his advisers. Such damage would have been permitted by them, only if they did not really want him to be the candidate for the Vice-presidency. Therefore, the Governor's advisors did not really want him to be such a candidate, if he actually signed the letter.

3–101. If the ceiling is not one thousand feet or above, you may not fly. If, and only if, the sequence report reads less than '10', the ceiling is below one thousand feet, since the last two zeros are always omitted. The sequence report, however, reads more than '10'. The conclusion is obvious: You may fly.

3–102. Evidently Joe is spelling words as they sound to him. I conclude this from the following facts: Only if he spells words as they sound to him will he spell 'trough' as 'troff'. If he spells words as they sound to him, he will spell 'didn't' as 'ding'. Now he never spells 'trough' as 'troff', but he always spells 'didn't' as 'ding'. See?

3–103. Plants X and Y can be crossed only if they are closely related. If their immediate parents have produced hybrids in the past, then X and Y cannot be crossed. Since their immediate parents have never produced hybrids, plants X and Y are closely related.

Necessary and Sufficient Conditions. **3–104 to 3–111.**

Take each conditional statement from each of the above arguments (3–96 to 3–103) and express it in the language of necessary and sufficient conditions. For convenience you may use the symbolization already assigned.

Other Major Types of Sentence Reasoning

Before examining some of the more difficult maneuvers in dealing with sentence reasoning, let us look at a few other basic types of statements that are made up of sentence units, and some elementary types of arguments in which they play a role. The words that are used to connect the unit sentences will be called 'LOGICAL OPERATORS'. 'If' and 'then', for example, are logical operators. Others are 'and', 'not both', 'either . . . , or'. It is these to which we now turn.

Reasoning using the conjunction 'and'

Very little needs to be said about conjunction. When we have a sentence of the form 'p and q', we can operate as if we had two sentences, one being 'p' and the other being 'q'. Each of these is called a conjunct, because they are joined by the conjunction 'and'. For example the following is a valid argument:

Example 3-25

If this object sinks in water, then it has a specific gravity greater than 1.
This object is made of brass and it sinks in water.
_____

This object has a specific gravity greater than 1.

When we treat the two conjuncts of the second premise independently, we can isolate the second conjunct and treat it as affirming the antecedent.

Conversely two separate assertions can be conjoined at our convenience. Here is an example of a valid argument in which this is the case:

Example 3-26

If Jones is a man and Jones is not yet married, then Jones is a bachelor.
Jones is a man.
Jones is not yet married.
_____

Jones is a bachelor.

In this case the antecedent consists of the conjunction of the last two premises, so we can treat the antecedent as having been affirmed when each of its conjuncts is separately affirmed. Incidentally, the antecedent would **not** have been affirmed had only one of the conjuncts been asserted.

Two conjuncts can be reordered without changing the meaning. In other words, '*p* and *q*' can be translated into '*q* and *p*'. This is in direct contrast to if-then sentences, where a reordering of sentences vitally affects the meaning.

Negajunction: 'not-both' reasoning

Sometimes one of the premises in an argument contains the words, 'not' and 'both'. Here is an example:

Example 3-27
It is not true that 'smearing' is both a noun and a verb in that sentence. 'Smearing' is a verb in that sentence.

'Smearing' is not a noun in that sentence.

The first premise can be viewed as two sentences, each of which I shall call a NEGAJUNCT, joined by logical operators. Representing these sentences by '*p*' and '*q*' as follows:

Let '*p*' = '"Smearing" is a noun in that sentence'
Let '*q*' = '"Smearing" is a verb in that sentence'

the premise can be symbolized as follows:

Not both *p* and *q*,

which might be rewritten in English as follows:

Not both of these are true: (a) 'Smearing' is a noun in that sentence, and (b) 'Smearing' is a verb in that sentence.

In this last formulation, which is equivalent to the first premise—although a bit longer, the sentences under consideration appear explicitly. Whenever you can make such a translation to something of the form of this last formulation, you are involved in NEGAJUNCTION.

The following form, AFFIRMING THE NEGAJUNCT, is valid:

Not both *p* and *q*
p

not *q*

The assertion of one of the negajuncts in 'not-both' reasoning requires the denial of the remaining negajunct. So, if the second premise were 'q', then the conclusion 'not p' could be validly drawn.

The following form, however, is **invalid**:

Not both p and q
Not p
_____

q

It is an invalid form because the premise says that it is not the case that both sentences are **true**; but this leaves open the possibility that they are both false, and it leaves open the possibility that one is true and the other false. Only one thing is ruled out: their both being true.

As with conjunction, the two sentences in the not-both relationship are interchangeable. That is, 'not both p and q' means the same as 'not both q and p'.*

This form, negajunction, is not translatable into a conditional relationship, although a negajunction is implied by a conditional relationship. That is,

'$p \longrightarrow q$' does imply 'Not both p and not q.'

Why? Think of it this way. Suppose 'If p, then q' is true; then one thing which we cannot have is 'p' true and 'q' false, for we know that if 'p' is true, then 'q' must be also true.

The reason that the converse ('not both p and not q' implies '$p \longrightarrow q$') does not hold is a difficult topic. Those who are interested may read something about it later in this chapter under the topic, "∴ Material Implication".

Alternation: 'either–or' reasoning**

Sentences which are joined by the logical operators, 'either' and 'or', are called alternations. Here are two examples:

This phenolphthalein solution will be pink, or it will be colorless.
Either Mark Twain intended to satirize local customs, or he was a foolish man.

---

* A qualification might be added here, and it might well have been added in the discussion of the interchangeability of conjuncts: This interchangeability is ordinarily a safe assumption, but it does ignore the time sequence in accord with which conjuncts and disjuncts are often arranged.

** A common practice among logicians nowadays is to reserve the title 'disjunction' for 'either-or' sentences, to which I assign the word 'alternation'. The terminology that I have adopted, because I think it to be more clear, is that used by Morris Cohen and Ernest Nagel in *An Introduction to Logic and Scientific Method* (New York: Harcourt, Brace and Company, 1934), and by Peter Strawson, *Introduction to Logical Theory* (London: Methuen and Company, Ltd., 1952).

Taking the second sentence, let us construct an argument making use of it:

Example 3-28
Either Mark Twain intended to satirize local customs, or he was a foolish man. Mark Twain clearly was not a foolish man.

_____

Therefore, Mark Twain intended to satirize local customs.

This argument can be symbolized as follows:

Let 'p' = 'Mark Twain intended to satirize local customs'
Let 'q' = 'he was a foolish man'

p or q
not q

_____

p

The argument is valid. If he was not a foolish man, then according to the first premise, he must have intended to satirize local customs. The above symbolization represents a valid form of argument using alternation.

Here is one way to see that the argument is valid: the alternation premise can be translated into either of the following conditional statements, which are contrapositives of each other:

If Mark Twain did not intend to satirize local customs, then he was a foolish man.
If Mark Twain was not a foolish man, then he intended to satirize local customs.

The addition of the second premise, "Mark Twain clearly was not a foolish man", to either of the conditional translations gives the conclusion, "Mark Twain intended to satirize local customs."

Unfortunately there is some controversy among logicians over whether such alternation statements also imply the converses of the above conditionals:

If Mark Twain was a foolish man, then he did not intend to satirize local customs.
If Mark Twain intended to satirize local customs, he was not a foolish man.

If the alternation also implies these conditionals, then it implies a biconditional and vice versa. The problem can be put symbolically: using the same symbols assigned for Example 3-28. Which of the following does 'p or q' mean, the conditional or the biconditional?

1. not $p \longrightarrow q$ (which is the same as 'not $q \longrightarrow p$'), or
2. not $p \longleftrightarrow q$ (which is the same as 'not $q \longleftrightarrow p$')

Another way to state the choices is to point out that according to the first interpretation, the affirmation of one alternant does not imply anything about the other, although the denial of either does imply the affirmation of the other. According to the second interpretation, the affirmation of either alternant implies the denial of the other, and the denial of either alternant implies the affirmation of the other. You can see that one's choice of these two interpretations of an alternation statement makes considerable difference in the judgment of alternation arguments.

The first interpretation, which is endorsed here, is called the WEAK 'OR' interpretation; the second the STRONG 'OR'. Many contemporary logicians endorse the weak 'or' interpretation, but with a qualification. They have a special definition of the conditional, which I will mention later on under the topic, "∴Material Implication". Another qualification holds for complex sentences. See that topic for this qualification.

An additional qualification exists which everyone should recognize—that sometimes when using the word 'or' people do intend that the affirmation of one alternant imply the negation of the other. This is often done by emphasizing the word 'or', which emphasis takes the place of the phrase 'but not both'. Consider this statement:

Either Frank put hydrochloric acid in that beaker, **or** he put in sulphuric acid.

The speaker seems to preclude Frank's having put both acids in the beaker.

Furthermore, features of the situation sometimes make clear that both alternants cannot be true at the same time. This is the case for the first alternation statement considered:

This phenolphthalein solution will be pink, or it will be colorless.

If any solution is pink, then it is not colorless, so the affirmation of one alternant in this case justifies denial of the other.

In view of these qualifications, an alternation statement sometimes implies that not both of the alternants are true. However, the safest thing to do, unless such an implication is absolutely clear, is to use the weak 'or' interpretation.

In evaluating an alternation argument, one proceeds by first determining whether the alternation is strong or weak. Given a strong alternation the following forms are **valid** (using '$\widehat{or}$' to represent the strong 'or'):

$$
\begin{array}{cccc}
p \;\widehat{or}\; q & p \;\widehat{or}\; q & p \;\widehat{or}\; q & p \;\widehat{or}\; q \\
\text{not } p & p & \text{not } q & q \\
\hline
q & \text{not } q & p & \text{not } p
\end{array}
$$

In each case the denial of the given conclusion (that is, not q, q, not p, and p respectively) would give us not only an invalid argument, but also a contradiction. Invalidity is rare with strong alternation and generally is the result of confusion when it does appear.

Given a weak alternation, the following two forms are **valid** (using simply the word 'or' for the symbol).

p or q	p or q
not p	not q
q	p

Or course the conclusions, 'not q' and 'not p' respectively cannot be validly drawn. The following forms are invalid:

p or q	p or q
p	q
not q	not p

And for the invalid forms, the conclusions, 'q' and 'p' respectively cannot be validly drawn either.

COMPREHENSION SELF-TEST

True or false? If the statement is false, change a crucial term (or terms) to make it true.

3–112. 'Not both p and not q' is a negajunction.

3–113. The affirmation of one negajunct implies the denial of the other.

3–114. The affirmation of one strong alternant implies the denial of the other.

3–115. The affirmation of one conjunct implies the denial of the other.

3–116. The denial of one weak alternant implies the affirmation of the other.

3–117. The affirmation of one weak alternant implies nothing about the other.

Symbolization Exercises. Symbolize each of the following sentences. Before writing the symbolized sentence, give a complete key.

3–118. This piece of cloth is warm and it is only 50 per cent wool.

3–119. This piece of cloth is warm, but it is only 50 per cent wool. (Note: For logical purposes, 'but' can often be treated like 'and'.)

3–120. Thomas Jefferson was a scholar; he was a gentleman; and he was an astute politician.

3–121. Either there will be rain within the week, or the crops will be ruined.

3–122. Either the two colors that you select will match, or the room will be ugly.

3–123. Either that figure is a square, or it does not have four sides.

3–124. There is not now both a rainbow and a completely overcast sky. (Or in other words—Not both of these are true: There is now a rainbow, and there is now a completely overcast sky.)

3–125. Either Abraham Lincoln thought that his Gettysburg Address was reverently received, or he thought that it was a failure.

3–126. *Alice in Wonderland* is a book for children, but it is also a book for adults.

3–127. Hamlet was not both in doubt of the guilt of his uncle and convinced that he had actually spoken to his father's ghost.

Translations. (**3–128** through **3–131**) Translate each of the four alternations in the previous group into equivalent conditionals.

Arguments to Judge. Here is a set of arguments. On a separate sheet of paper, symbolize each and put it in shape; then judge whether each is valid, explaining why you judge as you do.

3–132. This piece of cloth is warm and it is 50 per cent wool. If the dog is shivering from cold, then the cloth is not warm. Therefore the dog is not shivering from cold.

3–133. If the label on this piece of cloth reads "50 per cent wool", then it is 50 per cent wool. This morning John, who knows about such things, said that the piece of cloth is warm, but it is only 50 per cent wool. So the label certainly must read "50 per cent wool".

3–134. Thomas Jefferson did not make the mistake of which you are accusing him. If he had, then he would not have been an astute politician. But he was a scholar; he was a gentleman; and he was an astute politician.

3–135. Either there will be rain within the week, or the crops will be ruined. We can be sure that there will not be rain within the week. Hence we can be sure that the crops will be ruined.

3–136. Either the two colors that you select will match, or the room will be ugly. If I help you select the colors, then they will match. I am going to help you select the colors. Therefore, the room will not be ugly.

3–137. Either that figure is a square or it does not have four sides. I conclude that it does not have four sides, since I know that it is not a square.

3–138. There is not now both a rainbow and a completely overcast sky. The combination is impossible. The sky is now completely overcast. Therefore, you must be wrong when you say that there is now a rainbow.

3–139. Abraham Lincoln must have thought that his Gettysburg Address was a failure. The following reasons make this apparent: Either he thought that it was reverently received, or he thought that it was a failure. From his remarks made immediately afterwards, we can be sure that he did not think that it was reverently received.

3–140. If Jones likes *Alice in Wonderland*, then it is not a book for children. *Alice in Wonderland* is a book for children, but it is also a book for adults. Hence Jones probably likes it.

3–141. Hamlet must not have been in doubt of the guilt of his uncle. Consider: He certainly was not both in doubt of the guilt of his uncle and convinced that he had actually spoken to his father's ghost. Now he was convinced that he had actually spoken to his father's ghost. Hence in his mind there was no doubt of the guilt of his uncle.

❖Greater Complexities

Many topics in the field of logic are more complicated and sophisticated than the ones which you have considered so far. Although many of them have little bearing on the problems of ordinary logic, some are relevant. In this section you will confront a few of these topics which are relevant. One in particular, "Material Implication", touches on some of the basic controversies in contemporary logic. You should realize that at whatever level the subject matter of logic is presented, there are qualifications which for ease of presentation and understanding must be omitted. Consequently, although the topics in the remaining part of this chapter might be regarded as qualifications to what has already been presented, they too are also subject to a number of qualifications which are beyond the scope of this book.

∴Step-by-step organization of arguments

You have noted that arguments sometimes have a number of steps in reaching the conclusion. There is an orderly method for treating such arguments, a method which is particularly helpful with the more complex arguments. Recall this argument, used in an earlier exercise:

Example 3-29

If this figure is an equilateral triangle, then it has all sides equal.
I conclude that it cannot be an equilateral triangle, since not all sides are equal.

Let 'p' = 'this figure is an equilateral triangle'
Let 'q' = 'it has all sides equal'

In step-by-step form, the argument looks as follows:

Statements:	*Reasons:*
1. $p \rightarrow q$	1. Premise
2. not q	2. Premise
3. not p	3. 1, 2, denial of consequent

When using this procedure, you make two lists which correspond to each other and which are in order. The left-hand list consists of statements which you are entitled to make, granting the premises and truths of logic. The object is to be able to write down the conclusion in this list, but you may not write it unless previous items on the list, premises, and/or truths of logic entitle you to do so. Ordinarily you first write down all the premises. When you reach the conclusion and write it down, you have achieved the goal, so nothing appears after that step.

But if the argument is invalid, then it is not possible to get as far as writing down the conclusion. Instead, on the line after the last line that it is possible to establish, you write a question mark.

On the right-hand side you indicate just what it is that entitles you to make the statement written on the left. If the statement is a premise, then you write "premise". If the statement follows from earlier statements, you write down the numbers of the earlier statements and mention the rule of logic that enables you to make the step to this latest statement on the left.

In Example 3-29 above, the first two lines consist of the two premises (the conditional and the denial of the consequent of the conditional), and the word "premise" written on each line in order to indicate that each of the statements is a premise. The third line on the left consists of the denial of the antecedent, which is the proposed conclusion ('not p'); and on the right the numbers of the statements (1, 2) which justify this conclusion and an indication of the rule that entitles one to make this step.

In this case the rule, "denial of the consequent implies the denial of the antecedent", is indicated by the phrase, "denial of consequent". In referring to a rule, you generally mention the part that refers to what one of the premises does to the other. For a conditional chain, however, the thing to do is write down "conditional chain". In spite of the specificity of the previous two suggestions, you still have considerable leeway in the specification of reasons. As you will see, you will have to devise ways of indicating your reasons. This procedure is probably more conducive to understanding than using a set list of possible reasons, although it is less rigorous.

If the argument is invalid, then on the line on which the question mark is written, the reason should indicate to the extent possible why the argument is invalid. Here is an example of the step-by-step organization of an invalid argument:

Example 3-30

If these two plants are not closely related, then they cannot be crossed. However, they are closely related. Therefore, they can be crossed.

Let 'p' = 'these two plants are not closely related'
Let 'q' = 'these two plants cannot be crossed'

Statements:	Reasons:
1. $p \longrightarrow q$	1. Premise
2. not p	2. Premise
3. ?	3. 1, 2, denial of antecedent

Now that you have the general idea, let us apply this method of organization to a slightly more complex argument, which you have seen before. After you read the initial presentation of the argument in this one, try to work it all the way through yourself without looking at the way it is worked here. Then compare and see if the differences, if any, are crucial:

Example 3-31

I am convinced that the lighting in the livingroom is satisfactory. There can be no doubt about this, for it follows from the following reasons: If the lighting in the livingroom is indirect, then Mrs. Smith will like it. And one thing is clear— Mrs. Smith is a fair judge. If she does not like it, then it is clearly unsatisfactory. This morning she said that the lighting in the livingroom is indirect. My conclusion is therefore obvious.

Let 'p' = 'the lighting in the livingroom is indirect'
Let 'q' = 'Mrs. Smith will like it'

Let '*r*' = 'the lighting in the livingroom is unsatisfactory'

Statements:	*Reasons:*
1. $p \longrightarrow q$	1. Premise
2. not $q \longrightarrow r$	2. Premise
3. p	3. Premise
4. q	4. 1, 3, affirmation of antecedent
5. ?	5. 2, 4, denial of antecedent

Hence the argument is invalid.

This method of dealing with complex arguments presents a danger: There is no guarantee that you have exhausted all the possibilities for showing that an argument is valid. In a very complex argument there might be a way of showing that an argument is valid, but you might not see it. What this method does accomplish is the ordering of one's thoughts. It does not automatically grind out the answers. Such decision procedures do exist for some artificial systems of logic, but none exist for ordinary logic. You simply must be alert and ingenious.

COMPREHENSION SELF-TEST

True or False? If the statement is false, change a crucial term (or terms) to make it true.

3–142. In the step-by-step organization of arguments the object is to try to show that one is entitled to write down a premise as a last step.

3–143. In this method of organizing arguments, one thing that one is justified in writing down is a premise.

3–144. Ordinarily the first thing that one writes down in the step-by-step sequence is a premise.

3–145. In order to show what justifies a statement which is not a premise, one should indicate the lines from which it is derived and the rule by which it was derived.

Arguments to Organize and Judge. **3–146** through **3–165.** Take each of the following arguments from previous exercises, assign symbols (or make use of your previous assignment of symbols), organize it according to the step-by-step method, and state whether it is valid: 3–66, 3–67, 3–68, 3–69, 3–70, 3–96, 3–97, 3–98, 3–99, 3–100, 3–101, 3–102, 3–103, 3–135, 3–136, 3–137, 3–138, 3–139, 3–140, 3–141. If this practice becomes repetitive, leave out some of those in the middle.

3–166. Take the argument dealing with the relationship between the loss of the nail and the loss of the kingdom (Example 3–24) and organize it in step-by-step form.

❖Complex sentences

As may have occurred to you, each conditional, alternation, disjunction, and conjunction, although it is composed of sentences, is itself a sentence, and might be part of a more complex sentence, such as the following:

If you did put the yeast in the dough, then if the dough has rested in a warm place for thirty minutes, it has risen.

First, the assignment of symbols:

Let 'p' = 'you did put the yeast in the dough'
Let 'q' = 'the dough has rested in a warm place for thirty minutes'
Let 'r' = 'it has risen'

In this case, the conditional, '$q \rightarrow r$', is itself the consequent of the primary antecedent, 'p'. We can show this by enclosing the expression, '$q \rightarrow r$', in parentheses, and writing this all down after the 'p' and the arrow, as follows:

$$p \rightarrow (q \rightarrow r)$$

Here is an argument which makes use of this type of symbolization:

Example 3-32

If you did put the yeast in the dough, then if the dough has rested in a warm place for thirty minutes, it has risen. Now I know you put the yeast in the dough, but it has not risen. Therefore, the dough has not rested in a warm place for thirty minutes.

Since we have already assigned symbols to all the parts of this argument, we can turn to working it out in step-by-step form:

Statements:	*Reasons:*
1. $p \rightarrow (q \rightarrow r)$	1. Premise
2. p	2. Premise
3. not r	3. Premise
4. $q \rightarrow r$	4. 1, 2, affirmation of antecedent
5. not q	5. 3, 4, denial of consequent

Thus the argument is valid.

The thing that is new here is treating the simple conditional, '$q \rightarrow r$', as the consequent in the complex conditional, '$p \rightarrow (q \rightarrow r)$'. The affirmation of the antecedent 'p' in the complex conditional enables us to conclude the consequent of this complex conditional, which consequent is the simple conditional, '$q \rightarrow r$'.

Such complexities are not limited to conditional statements. The first premise in Example 3-32 can be restated to include an alternation:

If you did put the yeast in the dough; then either the dough has not rested in a warm place for thirty minutes, or it has risen.

Using the same assignment of letters, that sentence looks like this:

$$p \rightarrow (\text{not } q \text{ or } r)$$

Worked out in step-by-step form, the corresponding argument would look like this:

Example 3-33

Statements:	*Reasons:*
1. $p \longrightarrow$ (not q or r)	1. Premise
2. p	2. Premise
3. not r	3. Premise
4. not q or r	4. 1, 2, affirmation of antecedent
5. not q	5. 3, 4, denial of alternant

The thought can also be expressed in such a way that the antecedent is a conjunction:

If you did put the yeast in the dough and the dough has rested in a warm place for thirty minutes, then it has risen.

That sentence is symbolized as follows:

$$(p \text{ and } q) \longrightarrow r$$

Using this version of the complex premise, the argument looks like this:

Example 3-34

Statements:	*Reasons:*
1. $(p \text{ and } q) \longrightarrow r$	1. Premise
2. p	2. Premise
3. not r	3. Premise
4. not $(p \text{ and } q)$	4. 1, 3, denial of consequent
5. not q	5. 2, 4, affirmation of negajunct

You can now see that with the judicious use of parentheses, sentences of greater complexity can be handled. However, one should remember that the material in the parentheses must be treated as a unit which must be established before you can deal with its parts.* For example, the following move to line three is a mistake:

Example 3-35

Statements:	*Reasons:*
1. $p \longrightarrow (q \longrightarrow r)$	1. Premise
2. q	2. Premise
3. r	3. 1, 2, affirmation of antecedent

It is a mistake because the conditional that is presumed, '$q \longrightarrow r$', in arriving at 'r' has not been established.

---

* A qualification of this point is presented in the section on indirect proof, but for the sake of simplicity, it will be ignored here.

Next a qualification must be made to the earlier discussion of alternation, when it was suggested that an alternation can be translated into a conditional, and vice versa. That is, it was suggested that '$p \rightarrow q$' and 'not p or q' could be treated in the same way. This suggestion holds (assuming the weak 'or') for alternations that stand by themselves. But if the alternation is the antecedent of a conditional, then a proper interpretation of 'p or q' **can** be 'At least one of "p" and "q" is true.' Alternation with this interpretation will here be called INCLUSIVE ALTERNATION.

In the following sentence, the alternation is to be interpreted as inclusive alternation:

> If Smith is under thirty-five or he is an alien, then he is not eligible for the Presidency.

That sentence informs us that if at least one of the conditions is met, then Smith is ineligible. Thus in order to establish that the antecedent of the complete conditional is affirmed, one can establish that Smith is under thirty-five; alternatively one can establish that Smith is an alien. But one does not need to establish that there is a connection between the two alternants, which is what one would have to establish if the translation relationship between conditionals and alternations held in this kind of case.

Here is an argument put in step-by-step form, which shows how the affirmation of an inclusive alternant can be handled:

Example 3-36

If Smith is under thirty-five or he is an alien, then he is not eligible for the Presidency. Smith is an alien. Therefore, he is ineligible.

Let 'p' = 'Smith is under thirty-five'
Let 'q' = 'Smith is an alien'
Let 'r' = 'Smith is not eligible for the Presidency'

Statements:	*Reasons:*
1. $((p \text{ or } q)) \rightarrow r$	1. Premise
2. q	2. Premise
3. $(p \text{ or } q)$	3. 2, affirmation of inclusive alternant
4. r	4. 1, 3, affirmation of antecedent

The extra parentheses were put around the alternation in order to note the type of alternation in use here, inclusive alternation.

Probably one can safely say that whenever an alternation appears as a condition, it should be interpreted in this way. This is so for the above example in which the alternation was an antecedent that gives a condition, and it is so in the following example in which the alternant is a consequent that gives a condition by virtue of the 'only if' formulation:

> Jones may attend the banquet only if he has a varsity letter or he is to receive a trophy.

The person making the above statement would not be understood to be saying that Jones may attend only if there is a connection between having a varsity letter and being about to receive a trophy. Rather the statement would be taken to mean that Jones may attend only if he meets at least one of the conditions.

A word of warning: Our language is so complex that it is dangerous to rely exclusively on rules when you want to determine the meaning of a particular occurrence of the word 'or'. You can generally expect to find weak alternation when the alternation stands alone, although emphasis on the 'or' might make it strong alternation; and an alternation as a condition is generally to be interpreted as inclusive. But the final choice of one of the three interpretations must rest upon your appraisal of the context.

❖Indirect proof*

Frequently a proof is most conveniently constructed by assuming the proposed conclusion to be false and showing that this assumption leads to a contradiction. If the denial of the proposed conclusion leads to a contradiction, then the conclusion must be affirmed.

An understanding of the previous paragraph will enable you to deal effectively with most indirect proofs which you will meet. But in order that you can deal with complicated ones in an orderly manner, I will explain how to do so with the step-by-step method. Another purpose I hope to achieve in this section and the next one on conditional proofs is the appreciation on your part of the neatness and inescapability of even complicated deductive proofs.

In an indirect proof one first writes down the premises as usual. Then for the next step one writes down the denial of the proposed conclusion. Since the denial of the conclusion has not been established, but is simply assumed for the sake of argument, one indicates that it is an assumption by putting a star to its left. All succeeding steps up to and including the statement of a contradiction are similarly marked with the star, just to remind us that there is an assumption in the background.** We work for a contradiction, which should appear in the form, 'p and not p'. If we achieve a contradiction and it depends upon the assumption of the denial of the conclusion, then for the next step we can draw the conclusion. No star is necessary because the conclusion does not depend on the acceptance of the assumption.

Here is an example using the same argument as in Example 3-34:

---

* The procedure here adopted is modeled after that presented by W. V. Quine, *Methods of Logic* (New York: Holt-Dryden, 1959).

** One could star only those steps which actually depend on the assumption, but it is simpler to star all statements that are made up through the contradiction. Since this procedure does no harm and is simpler, it is used here.

Example 3-37

Statements:	*Reasons:*
1. (p and q) $\longrightarrow r$	1. Premise
2. p	2. Premise
3. not r	3. Premise
*4. q	4. Assumption
*5. r	5. 2, 4, 1, affirmation of antecedent
*6. r and not r	6. 5, 3
7. not q	7. 4, 6, indirect proof

On the assumption, 'q', we conclude 'r'. But we are given 'not r' as a premise, so we have a contradiction, 'r and not r'. Hence the assumption, 'q', must be false. Hence we can conclude 'not q'. The argument is valid.

The basic idea behind indirect proof is roughly the principle that the denial of the consequent implies the denial of the antecedent. In the starred part of the proof one tries to show that if the conclusion is false, then there is a contradiction. Since a contradiction must be denied, the falsity of the conclusion must also be denied. To deny the falsity of the conclusion is to affirm it.

The above example of an indirect proof is very simple and saved no steps in that particular argument. In fact it required more steps than the direct method. But there are times, as you will see in the exercises, that the indirect method is simpler and easier to see.

Sometimes indirect proofs become quite complicated. For example, on occasion one must make an assumption within a sequence that is already starred. To do this calls for double starring in order that we be reminded of the new assumption. This sort of thing is rather rare, though, so the simple procedure of starring which is exemplified above will handle most cases.

∴Proving a conditional

The techniques which you have learned earlier enable you to judge some conclusions which are **themselves** conditionals. But unless there is a conditional chain or the conditional appears as a unit in one of the premises, you probably do not yet see how to handle such things. Consider this argument:

Example 3-38

If Congress passes that bill, then it will be ruled on by the Supreme Court, if, and only if, someone contests it. It is clear that if the Supreme Court rules on the bill, it will be declared unconstitutional. It is also clear that someone will contest it. Therefore, if Congress passes the bill, it will be declared unconstitutional.

First the assignment of symbols:

Let 'p' = 'Congress passes the bill'
Let 'q' = 'it will be ruled on by the Supreme Court'
Let 'r' = 'someone contests it'
Let 's' = 'it will be declared unconstitutional'

Next the first steps:

Statements:	Reasons:
1. $p \longrightarrow (q \longleftrightarrow r)$	1. Premise
2. $q \longrightarrow s$	2. Premise
3. r	3. Premise

But now what? How can we work toward the conclusion, '$p \longrightarrow s$'? One strategy that can be used is to assume the antecedent of the conclusion and see if we can derive the consequent. If we can, then we have established the conclusion, for we have shown that if the antecedent is true, then the consequent is true.

Here is the rest of the step-by-step working out of the argument, again making use of the starring procedure to remind us of the assumption that is in the background in deriving the consequent of the conclusion. In the step after the one in which the consequent is derived, the star is omitted, because this step, in which the conclusion is stated (step 8), does not itself depend upon the assumption:

*4. p	4. Assumption
*5. $q \longleftrightarrow r$	5. 4, 1, affirmation of antecedent
*6. q	6. 3, 5, affirmation of one side of a biconditional
*7. s	7. 6, 2, affirmation of antecedent
8. $p \longrightarrow s$	8. 4, 7, conditional proof
The argument is valid.	

The starred steps show that if p, then s, which is the desired conclusion. So we are entitled to write down the desired conclusion at step 8.

COMPREHENSION SELF-TEST

True or False? If the statement is false, change a crucial term (or terms) to make it true.

3–167. An indirect proof starts by assuming the truth of the conclusion.

3–168. The method of indirect proof is similar in spirit to the valid form, denying the consequent.

3–169. If one conditional is the antecedent of another, then for purposes of symbolizing the complex whole, the first conditional is enclosed in parentheses.

3–170. In order to show that something has been proven in an indirect proof, one puts a star to the left of each line that has been proven.

3–171. The following constitutes a proof of a conditional: The antecedent is assumed and the consequent is shown to follow thereby.

Sentences to Symbolize. Put each of the following sentences into the symbolic form that most closely adheres to the way the sentence is actually stated. Give a key to your assignment of symbols in each case.

3–172. If Governor Smith is actually planning to throw his hat in the ring; then if the reporters asked him to declare himself, he has refused to do so.

3–173. If Governor Smith is actually planning to throw his hat in the ring; then either the reporters did not ask him to declare himself, or he has refused to do so.

3–174. If Governor Smith is actually planning to throw his hat in the ring, and the reporters asked him to declare himself; then he has refused to do so.

3–175. If Iceland has ordered the fishing vessels of Great Britain to leave the area within ten miles of Iceland's shores; then Iceland is sovereign in that ten-mile zone, only if the ships of Britain leave.

3–176. If Iceland has ordered the fishing vessels of Great Britain to leave the area within ten miles of Iceland's shores; then Iceland is sovereign in that ten-mile zone, if the ships of Britain leave.

3–177. If Jones is given the *California Test of Mental Maturity* under standard conditions; then his IQ is about 100, if, and only if, his score is about 100.

3–178. If you put this mercury thermometer in the beaker of water; then the thermometer read x, if, and only if, the temperature was x.

3–179. Either this small test piece of dough, if put in the warming pan, will at least double in size in twenty minutes, or the dough on the board will not rise sufficiently if put in the oven.

3–180. If lines AB and CD were not parallel to each other; then if a third line is drawn in the same plane, either it will cross one and only one of them, or it will cross both of them.

Arguments to Judge. Here is a set of arguments. On a separate sheet of paper, check their validity using the step-by-step method. Make sure that your assignment of symbols is clear. In each case state explicitly whether the argument is valid.

3–181. The reporters did not ask Governor Smith to declare himself. Here is why I think so: If Governor Smith is actually planning to throw his hat in the ring; then if the reporters did ask him to declare himself, he has refused to do so. Now I know from the Governor's own testimony that he is planning to throw his hat in the ring, but that he has not refused to declare himself.

3–182. If Iceland has ordered the fishing vessels of Great Britain to leave the area within ten miles of Iceland's shores; then Iceland is sovereign in that ten-mile zone only if the ships of Britain leave. Iceland has made such an order, and the ships of Britain left. Hence Iceland is sovereign in the area within ten miles of its shores.

3–183. If Jones is given the *California Test of Mental Maturity* under standard conditions; then his IQ is about 100, if, and only if, his score is about 100. Jones does not both know calculus and have an IQ of 100. But he does know calculus and his score on the test was 100. Hence Jones was not given the test under standard conditions.

3-184. If you put this mercury thermometer in the beaker of water; then the thermometer read x, if, and only if, the temperature was x. You did put this mercury thermometer in the water and it read x. Hence the temperature of the water was x.

3-185. Let me describe the test for the rising ability of the dough on the board: Either this small test piece of dough, if put in the warming pan, will at least double in size in twenty minutes, or the dough on the board will not rise sufficiently if put in the oven. The test piece did not double in size in twenty minutes, though it was put in the warming pan. The dough on the board is in the oven. Therefore, it will not rise sufficiently.

3-186. If lines AB and CD are not parallel to each other; then if a third line has been drawn in the same plane, either it will cross one and only one of them, or it will cross both of them. A third line has been drawn in the same plane, and it crosses neither AB nor CD. Hence lines AB and CD are parallel.

3-187. If X was rubbed on Y; then X is harder than Y, if, and only if, X scratched Y. Only if there are marks on Y did X scratch Y. X was rubbed on Y, and there are clear marks on Y. Therefore, X is harder than Y.

3-188. If this pronoun is the object of a preposition, then it requires the objective form. If it requires the objective form, then it should appear as 'him'. If it appears as 'he' and it should appear as 'him', then the sentence is in error. Hence the sentence is in error, if the pronoun appears as 'he', and is the object of a preposition.

3-189. If Communism were going to spread in Lower Slobbovia, then the Prime Minister would have been defeated in the recent election. He has been defeated, only if there has been an announcement of his defeat in the local newspaper. No mention of such a defeat has been made, nor will it appear. On the basis of inside information, I know for a fact that the Lower Slobbovians are discontent. On the basis of the foregoing, I conclude that the following statement is false: If the people of Lower Slobbovia are discontent, then Communism will spread in Lower Slobbovia.

3-190. The wind is not from the east. If, and only if, the contour lines are close together, is the hill steep. If the hill is steep, then there is undoubtedly turbulence on the west side, if the wind is from the west. We shall not have both turbulence on the west side and a good race close to the west shore. We must have our race on a triangular course with two buoys on the east shore, if we shall not have a good race close to the west shore. The contour lines **are** quite close together. Therefore, if the wind is from the west, then we must have our race on a triangular course with two buoys on the east shore.

❖Material implication

So far I have assumed that a conditional statement suggests some kind of connection between an antecedent and consequent. If one does not make this assumption, then the logical system that one constructs can be much simpler—in that fewer basic relationships need be assumed (though it will not be simpler from the point of view of ease of understanding, as parts of the system appear to be counterintuitive).

Most contemporary symbolic logicians have chosen not to make this assumption of a connection between the antecedent and consequent, and have worked on the construction of elegant* systems of logic. Although they realize that the systems so constructed are somewhat artificial, many do so anyway because of the attraction of such systems.

This section on material implication is intended only to point out some basic features of many contemporary systems. Although various systems differ from each other in many ways, they do share the features presented here. Unless you are interested in these matters for their own sake, or are planning to go on in your study of logic, I suggest that you omit this section. It will not be of additional help to you in judging deductive arguments that are used in everyday life.

Since this topic is presumably of interest only to those who have found the material so far rather easy, the discussion that follows will be compact. P. F. Strawson in his *Introduction to Logical Theory*** has treated the topic at much greater length. Those who are interested are urged to go to Strawson's book and to some of the other items in the bibliography,*** because what follows here is sketchy and in need of qualification.

The basic feature of the approach is revealed by the definition of the conditional:

'If p, then q' means the same as 'Not both p and not q'.

In this definition the conditional is equated to a negajunction, which is a combination of negation and conjunction. As the negajunction is interpreted, it is made true by the falsity of either one of its components. There is at least some plausibility in this equation, because the conditional does imply that negajunction. If it is true that if p, than q; then it cannot be that p is true and q is false. But the trouble is that the negajunction does not imply the conditional. This is shown by the fact that the negajunction is made true by things which do not make the conditional true. So the negajunction can be true when the conditional is not. If the negajunction implied the conditional, this could not be.

To see that the negajunction is made true by things which do not make the conditional true, consider just what can make the negajunction true. The negajunction that appears in the above definition is made true by the

---

* 'Elegant' is not here a derogatory term. Rather it is laudatory.
** *Op. cit.*
*** At the end of Chapter 5.

falsity of '*p*' or the truth of '*q*'. Thus according to this interpretation the **defined conditional** is made true by the falsity of '*p*' or the truth of '*q*'. This is a special kind of conditional and is called the MATERIAL CONDITIONAL. The if-then relationship so defined is called MATERIAL IMPLICATION.

That material implication is special can be seen from this example of a conditional:

If I go to lunch at 2:00 P.M. today, there will be a broad selection of food.

Interpreted as material implication, this conditional is made true by the falsity of the antecedent. That is, the conditional is true if I do **not** go to lunch at 2:00 P.M. today. Under the ordinary interpretation of this conditional, however, I happen to know that the statement is false. I know that if I go to lunch at 2:00 P.M. today, there will be a small selection. And I know this to be so even if I do not go to lunch at 2:00 P.M. today. Hence the material conditional is different from the ordinary conditional.

The problem is compounded by the fact that all conditionals are interpreted as material conditionals (or in similar ways) in the views under consideration. So there is no room for the ordinary conditional.

A number of parallel situations can be pointed out: The word 'or' is interpreted in the inclusive sense; everything is supposed to be true of any class which has no members; and in fact there is supposed to be only one such class. But there is not space here to discuss each of these matters. If you would like to pursue them, you can find expositions of the positions in many contemporary books on logic. Your understanding of them will perhaps be facilitated by the above discussion of material implication.

Now that you have seen the consequences of this particular definition of the conditional, you might wonder why anyone should desire to so define it. There are several reasons:

1. As was indicated earlier, such a definition allows one to construct a much more elegant system than the one I have presented. Starting with fewer (usually two) independent logical operators, one can define all other operators in sentence reasoning. Thus there are fewer types of building blocks. Sometimes conjunction and negation are the two; sometimes inclusive alternation and negation are the two. As a matter of fact one can start with only one operator (negajunction will do it) and define all the rest.

2. Such a definition allows the development of a convenient mechanical decision procedure for judging arguments. Perhaps you have heard of truth tables. They are used in one such procedure.

3. The difficulties which I have indicated do not often give trouble in practical situations, and when they do, one who is on guard might not be caught in the traps.

4. The defined relationship, material implication, is not very far removed from our intuitive notion of implication. After all, '$p \rightarrow q$' does imply 'Not both p and not q', and when 'Not both p and not q' is established on grounds other than the falsity of p or the truth of q, the relationship '$p \rightarrow q$' holds.

These are important considerations, but I have still chosen to give you a logic that assumes that conditionals assert connections, primarily because this logic is intuitive and correct. The elegance of modern systems is not of much help when dealing with the problems of everyday logic.

Chapter Summary

In this chapter on sentence reasoning, you have seen in some detail the role of conditional statements in arguments. The fundamental valid types of conditional arguments are called **affirming the antecedent, denying the consequent,** and the **conditional chain**. The fundamental invalid forms are **denying the antecedent** and **affirming the consequent**. A crucial distinction is that between the antecedent and the consequent. They must not be exchanged when dealing with conditionals.

The only-if type of conditional is rather confusing in this respect, because the words 'only if' introduce the consequent—in contrast to the introduction of the antecedent by the word 'if' in the standard 'if-then' statement.

The move from a statement to its converse is not a valid move, but the move to its contrapositive is valid and often helpful in organizing arguments. In general the denial of the negation of a statement may be treated as equivalent to the straightforward affirmation of it.

Sometimes one's insight into the nature of an argument is helped by thinking in terms of necessary and sufficient conditions. In the symbolic form, '$p \rightarrow q$', the truth of 'p' is a sufficient condition for the truth of 'q', and the truth of 'q' is a necessary condition for the truth of 'p'.

The biconditional, a statement of implication in both directions, is conveniently indicated by the phrase, 'if, and only if'. It is difficult to make a mistake in reasoning with biconditionals because valid arguments can be developed out of the affirmation or denial of the antecedent or consequent. The main danger is in confusion with negation.

Conjunction, the joining together of two statements by the conjunction 'and' (or some similar one), offers few problems. A conjunction is true, if, and only if, both conjuncts are true. The order of the conjuncts does not matter.

Negajunction, the denial of a conjunction, is a bit more confusing because of the negation. The order of the parts in the negajunction also does not matter. A negajunction is true, if, and only if, at least one of the negajuncts is false. Negajunctions and conjunctions do not express connections between their parts—or at least we so treat them.

There appear to be at least three significant types of alternation: weak alternation, strong alternation, and (∴) inclusive alternation. Weak alternation is translatable into a conditional, strong alternation into a biconditional, and inclusive alternation into the statement that at least one of the alternants is true. The decision as to which type is in use rests heavily on the context, although inclusive alternation (while the alternants are sentences) probably does not appear except as part of a complex sentence, usually in which the alternation plays the role of a condition.

The basic units of sentence reasoning are symbolized by representing them by small letters, '*p*', '*q*', etc. The conditional, biconditional, conjunction, negajunction, and alternation relationships are respectively symbolized by '→', '↔', 'and', 'not both . . . and . . .', and 'or'. A circle is drawn around the 'or' ('ⓞⓡ') to show that the alternation is strong, and (∴) parentheses are put around the entire alternation if it is inclusive alternation.

The last section in this chapter, "Greater Complexities", is devoted to advanced material and considers five topics: "Step-by-Step Organization of Arguments", "Complex Sentences", "Indirect Proof", "Proving a Conditional", and "Material Implication".

∴When arguments are long and complicated, an orderly step-by-step method has been suggested. When following this method, one lists on the left the premises and what one is entitled to conclude on the basis of the premises; on the right are given the reasons for the entitlement to write what is written on the left. Indirect proofs are handled by assuming the denial of the proposed conclusion, and by seeking to derive a contradiction from this assumption. The assumption, contradiction, and intervening lines are starred in order to keep track of what is going on. Conditional proofs (proofs of conditional statements) are sometimes effected by assuming the antecedent of the conditional and seeing if one can derive the consequent. Again starring is used to keep track of the basis on which one is proceeding. The step-by-step method does not guarantee that one will find that a valid argument is valid. Considerable ingenuity must sometimes be exercised.

∴Complex statements can be symbolized by using parentheses to show the grouping of their parts. For example 'If *p*; then if *q*, then *r*' can be symbolized as $p \rightarrow (q \rightarrow r)$. The parentheses show that '$q \rightarrow r$' is to be taken as a unit in the total conditional.

∴The last topic in the chapter dealt with contemporary artificial logic systems, although no effort was made to achieve comprehensive coverage. Instead, a crucial but typical difference was briefly described. This difference is the definition of the conditional in terms of a negajunction.

Lastly you should remember that this chapter has dealt with only one kind of logic, that in which the basic units are sentences which remain essentially unchanged throughout the argument. The next chapter treats class reasoning, in which sentences change radically during the course of the argument. In some cases similar techniques can be used, but often the easiest way is to use circles to represent classes. We now turn to this method.

CHAPTER 4

Class Reasoning

You have seen what deduction is and found some techniques for handling deductive arguments in which the logical operators joined complete independent sentences or items that could be treated as such. This chapter is concerned with another sort of argument, that in which the basic units are individuals and classes, rather than sentences. Class reasoning arguments, like sentence arguments, are very common, so you should also know how to handle them.

You will find that class and sentence reasoning are related in various ways. Frequently they are combined in the same argument; some arguments can be shifted from one type to the other without serious change in meaning; and like all deductive arguments, they involve the basic relationship, which is here stated in conditional form: **If** the premises are true and the argument is valid **then** the conclusion must be true.

But each is uniquely suited to certain jobs. Class reasoning cannot handle most of the arguments considered in the previous chapter, because no classes were involved—only specific things and events. And sentence reasoning is not well suited to the following two arguments (although you can handle the first with sentence reasoning either by overlooking a difficulty, or by adding a special step). Examine these two arguments, which are valid, and see whether you can show that they are valid, using the techniques of sentence reasoning:

Example 4-1
Dough containing yeast mixed with lukewarm water rises rapidly.
Ingrid's dough contains yeast mixed with lukewarm water.

Ingrid's dough rises rapidly.

Example 4-2
All triangles inscribed in semi-circles are right triangles.
At least some of the triangles on this page are inscribed in semi-circles. [A geome-
try text]

At least some of the triangles on this page are right triangles.

You may have had a degree of success with the first argument, but you surely
did not succeed with the second one. You might have done this with the
first argument:

Example 4-3
Let 'p' = 'any dough contains yeast mixed with lukewarm water'
Let 'q' = 'that dough rises rapidly'

$p \longrightarrow q$
p
q (valid; affirmation of the antecedent)

In so doing we have restated the first premise to read:

If any dough contains yeast mixed with lukewarm water, then that dough rises
rapidly,

which is a fairly satisfactory restatement of the first premise. But note that
what was affirmed was not the antecedent, "any dough contains yeast mixed
with lukewarm water", but rather the sentence, "Ingrid's dough contains
yeast mixed with lukewarm water." In fact it would not make sense to affirm
the antecedent of the revised if-then sentence, because that sentence fails to
refer to some dough. If you do not know what dough is referred to, how can
you tell whether it contains yeast mixed with lukewarm water? Incidentally
the second premise, "Ingrid's dough contains yeast mixed with lukewarm
water", does refer to some particular dough, so it does make sense to affirm
that.

Example 4-2, the one which concluded, "At least some of the triangles
on this page are right triangles", is not at all amenable to the sentence approach. It can, however, be handled by a class reasoning approach. Although
many ways of doing class reasoning may be found in the literature on logic,
the one that you will read about here is probably the simplest and most
intuitive. It has the additional advantage of being usable at various levels
of sophistication. If a person knows just a little of it, he can make use of that.

A complicated set of techniques need not be mastered before the simplest problems can be worked.

A Simple Euler Circle System

The system you are about to study is a modification of a circle system named after Leonhard Euler, a Swiss mathematician who developed his system in order to teach deductive logic to a German princess. The basic idea is to represent a class by the area bounded by a circle actually drawn with a writing implement on a surface. All the members of the class can be treated as being **inside** that circle.

This Euler circle system is to some extent similar to another circle system —the Venn diagram system. The latter is more formal and invites difficulties that parallel the difficulties of material implication mentioned in the last chapter. Some contemporary instruction in modern mathematics makes use of a system which is called "Venn Diagrams", but which actually is a combination of the Euler and Venn approaches. I shall not examine the pure Venn approach in this chapter; if you are curious, you can find it presented in many elementary logic texts.

For purposes of simplicity in presentation of this Euler system, I shall postpone consideration of the triangle example and commence with the dough example.

Let us proceed to represent this argument with circles. Consider the first premise. "Dough containing yeast mixed with lukewarm water rises rapidly." In effect it says that the class of dough* containing yeast mixed with lukewarm water (the subject of the sentence) is included in the class of dough that rises rapidly. It is represented by assigning a circle to each class and putting the circle for the subject class inside the circle for the predicate class (See Diagram 4-1). This diagram says:

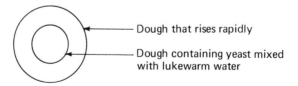

DIAGRAM 4-1

---

* For purposes of simplicity, I am ignoring the distinction between general terms and class terms. Strictly speaking, dough containing yeast mixed with lukewarm water is not a class, although pieces of such dough are a class. One can imagine each use of a general term to be so converted for purposes of fitting the circle model.

All of the members of the class, *dough containing yeast mixed with lukewarm water*, are also members of the class, *dough that rises rapidly*.

Consider the second premise, "Ingrid's dough contains yeast mixed with lukewarm water." It is diagramed similarly (see Diagram 4-2). This diagram says:

Ingrid's dough is a member of the class, *dough containing yeast mixed with lukewarm water*.

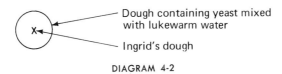

Dough containing yeast mixed with lukewarm water

Ingrid's dough

DIAGRAM 4-2

The cross, instead of a circle, was used to represent Ingrid's dough because that is not a class in this context; it is a single thing. For some situations you can ignore this distinction and use circles to bound single things as well as groups of things, but please adhere to the distinction for present purposes. It is of theoretical importance.*

Now let us combine the two premises in a single diagram. They share a circle in common so we can put them together. A good strategy is to so select your classes that the premises have circles in common. When combined the two premises look like those in Diagram 4-3. Inescapably the cross

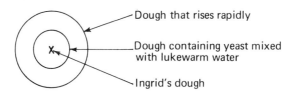

Dough that rises rapidly

Dough containing yeast mixed with lukewarm water

Ingrid's dough

DIAGRAM 4-3

representing Indrid's dough is within the boundary of the class of dough that rises rapidly. That is, inescapably Ingrid's dough is a member of the class, *dough that rises rapidly*. Thus the conclusion is inescapably represented in the diagram and the argument is valid.

* The distinction between class membership and class inclusion, which is emphasized in set theory, is thereby preserved.

General strategy

We have now worked through one argument, applying the circle-method validity test. The general strategy to follow is this:

Try to represent the premises in one diagram. Seek common classes in different premises and take advantage of these classes to combine the premises. At all times work against the conclusion. If the conclusion is inescapably represented in the combined diagram, then the argument is valid.

In the previous argument, we were forced by one premise to put the '*x*' for Ingrid's dough inside the circle for dough containing yeast mixed with lukewarm water, and we were forced by another premise to put the latter circle inside the circle for dough that rises rapidly. Thus there was no way out. The conclusion was inescapably represented by the combined diagram.

Here is a second example of the same logical form:

Example 4-4
All of the chairs in this room are wooden.
All wooden things can burn.
_____
All of the chairs in this room can burn.

Again the sentences must be transformed either explicitly or implicitly to fit the class relationship pattern. A predicate class must be created, and it must be connected to the subject by means of the verb, 'to be'. I shall repeat the argument, making the transformations explicit for purposes of illustration. You need not rewrite each sentence every time you check an argument, but you must think in terms of classes. Here is the transformed argument with the class relationships made explicit and the classes in italics:

Example 4-5
All *the chairs in this room* are *wooden things.*
All *wooden things* are *things that can burn.*
_____
All *the chairs in this room* are *things that can burn.*

As you can see, the explicitly transformed sentences are somewhat stilted, but there is no doubt about their meaning. After you check the validity you can change back again.

Now that you have the transformed sentences in front of you, it would be a good idea for you to get out a piece of paper and pencil and check the argument by means of the Euler circle system. When you finish, your diagram should look like Diagram 4-4.

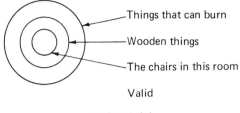

Things that can burn

Wooden things

The chairs in this room

Valid

DIAGRAM 4-4

COMPREHENSION SELF-TEST

True or False? If the statement is false, change a crucial term (or terms) to make it true.

4–1. In the Euler circle system, a sentence is represented by a circle.

4–2. In a sentence of the form, "All *A*'s are *B*'s", the circle for the *B*'s would be put inside the circle for the *A*'s.

4–3. A singular thing, as opposed to a class, is represented by an '*x*'.

Diagrams. Here are a number of sentences. Using what you know so far about the modified Euler system, represent each sentence with an Euler diagram. Label each diagram. Remember that in some cases you will have to construct a predicate class.

4–4. All parallelograms are quadrilaterals.

4–5. All quadrilaterals are plane figures.

4–6. All of the books by Thomas Mann are on the top shelf.

4–7. Every one of Chekhov's short stories has fascinated me.

4–8. All acids are compounds.

4–9. All the stars in the Milky Way are far away.

4–10. Every state has two senators.

4–11. All unwanted plants are weeds.

Arguments to Diagram. The following arguments are all valid. For each argument make a labeled diagram that will show that the argument is valid.

4–12. All parallelograms are quadrilaterals. All quadrilaterals are plane figures. Therefore, all parallelograms are plane figures.

4–13. *Magic Mountain* is by Thomas Mann. All of the books by Thomas Mann are on the top shelf. Hence *Magic Mountain* is on the top shelf.

4–14. All literary works that have fascinated me have had an influence on my life. Since all of Chekhov's short stories have fascinated me, they have all had an influence on my life.

4–15. All acids are compounds and all compounds are composed of more than one element. Hence all acids are composed of more than one element.

4–16. Heavenly bodies that are far away have little or no influence on the course of events in the world. Since all of the stars in the Milky Way are far away, they do not have much influence on the course of events in the world. (Do not be concerned with the truth of the statements; just pay attention to their meaning and the logical relationships.)

4–17. Every state has two senators. Whatever has two senators has two important votes in treaty ratification. Hence every state has two important votes in treaty ratification.

4–18. All unwanted plants are weeds. The wheat in my cornfield is unwanted. Hence the wheat in my cornfield is a weed.

Invalidity

Let us turn to an invalid argument to see how its invalidity is exposed by this Euler circle system:

Example 4-6
All of the chairs in this room can burn.
All wooden things can burn.
_____
All of the chairs in this room are wooden.

Since this is such a simple argument, you can probably see already that it is invalid, because the premises allow that the chairs burn because they are made of some other material.

Remember the strategy: work against the conclusion. In this case you find that diagraming the premises does not commit one inescapably to diagraming the conclusion. An easy way to show this is to show some of the possibilities that are left open by the premises, at least one of which possibilities is inconsistent with the conclusion. Appropriately placed question marks make this situation clear (see Diagram 4-5). The circle for the chairs in this

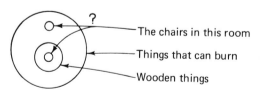

The chairs in this room
Things that can burn
Wooden things

DIAGRAM 4-5

room must be in the things-that-can-burn circle, but it might or might not be in the wooden-things circle. Two of the possibilities are shown by two possible different placements of the circle for the chairs in this room.

COMPREHENSION SELF-TEST

True or False? If the statement is false, change a crucial term (or terms) to make it true.

4–19. If an argument is invalid, then it is possible to diagram the premises without diagraming the conclusion.

4–20. If an argument is valid, a diagraming of the premises inescapably results in a diagraming of the conclusion.

4–21. It is here recommended that the invalidity of an argument be shown by diagraming the argument in two ways, one of which does not represent the conclusion.

Arguments to Diagram and Judge. Here is a set of arguments, some of which are invalid. Diagram each argument, labeling each circle or '*x*', judge the validity, and show by the suggested means that the invalid arguments are invalid.

4–22. All triangles with two equal sides are isosceles triangles. Triangle *ABC* has two equal sides. Therefore, triangle *ABC* is an isosceles triangle.

4–23. All nearsighted people have defective eyes. John's eyes are defective. Hence John is nearsighted.

4–24. Birds that are unable to fly are fast runners. The penguin is a bird that is unable to fly. Therefore, the penguin is a fast runner.

4–25. Indices used to show trends in productivity should take into account changes in the cost of living. The index (percent increase in the Gross National Product) is used to show trends in productivity. Therefore, that index should take into account changes in the cost of living.

4–26. Wool clothing is warm. Clothing that is worn in winter is warm. Therefore, wool clothing is worn in winter.

4–27. The first few sentences in Mark Antony's speech to the people of Rome should be combined, because these sentences are short, and short sentences should always be combined.

4–28. The practice of lay investiture was a practice that weakened the church. Any practice weakening the church was opposed by the papacy. Hence the practice of lay investiture was opposed by the papacy.

4–29. An equilateral polygon inscribed in a circle is a regular polygon. *ABCDE* is a regular polygon. Therefore, it is an equilateral polygon inscribed in a circle.

Negatives

If we want to show that no members of a given class are members of another class, the two circles are drawn apart from each other. For example the sentence, 'No past-presidents are women', would look like Diagram 4-6. As you can see, that would also represent the equivalent sentence, 'No women have been president'.

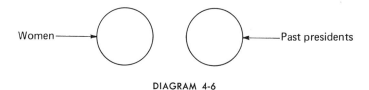

DIAGRAM 4-6

Consider this argument which uses the above sentence as a premise:

Example 4-7

No women have been president.
W. H. Harrison was a president.
_____

W. H. Harrison was not a woman.

The diagram of this valid argument (Diagram 4-7) is such that there is no way to put W. H. Harrison into the circle for women; hence the argument is valid.

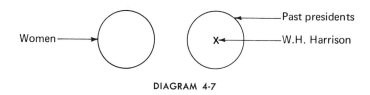

DIAGRAM 4-7

Transformations among negatives and positives*

Sometimes in dealing with arguments, one must transform a sentence from negative form to positive form, or vice versa. Doing this is made easy by reference to Euler diagrams, but a new concept must be used, *the universe of discourse*. In effect, the UNIVERSE OF DISCOURSE is an encompassing class

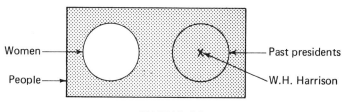

DIAGRAM 4-8

* For purposes of simplicity I shall neglect the problem of possible nonexistence of members of the subject and predicate classes. One's own grasp of the context is sufficient for proper treatment of any difficulties.

which includes members and nonmembers of all the classes involved in an argument or sentence. For example, a possible universe of discourse for the argument dealing with presidents is people. This can be shown by drawing a large rectangle around everything and labeling it 'people'. Now according to this convention, the area inside the circle labeled 'women' represents women and the area outside this circle (shaded area) represents nonwomen (who are people). Thus Diagram 4-8 shows the division of the universe of discourse, people, into two classes, women and nonwomen. Since the circle for past presidents is part of the shaded area, this diagram says that all past presidents are nonwomen (or are not women). It also says that W. H. Harrison was a nonwoman (was not a woman), since the 'x' for W. H. Harrison is in the past-president circle, which in turn must be in the shaded area.

Now let us shade the diagram so that our attention is focused on the two mutually exclusive classes, past presidents and nonpast presidents.

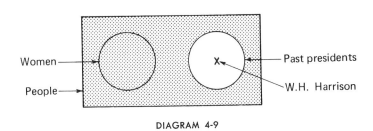

DIAGRAM 4-9

The area enclosed by the circle labeled 'past presidents' represents past presidents and the area outside this circle (shaded area) represents nonpast-presidents (who are people). Since the circle for women is part of the shaded area, Diagram 4-9 clearly says that all women are nonpast presidents, or in other words, are not past presidents.

The fact that the following sentences are all equivalent may thus be read off the original diagram (Diagram 4-7):

No past presidents are women.
No women have been president.
All past presidents are nonwomen (or are not women).
All women are nonpast presidents (or are not past presidents).

You perhaps did not need diagrams to make those transformations, but I deliberately chose a simple example to make the procedure clear. The next example is more difficult.

Perhaps you are not aware that the following two sentences are equivalent:

All wooden things can burn.
All nonburnable things are not wooden.

This can be shown by an Euler diagram (Diagram 4-10) with a universe of discourse. As an aid to your imagination I have redrawn the diagram

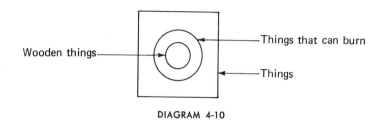

DIAGRAM 4-10

twice. The first time (Diagram 4-11) the nonwooden things are shaded. The second time (Diagram 4-12) the nonburnable things are shaded. You

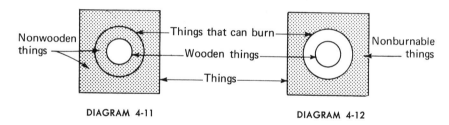

DIAGRAM 4-11   DIAGRAM 4-12

will see that the area for nonburnable things is included in the area for nonwooden things and thus that the sentence, 'All nonburnable things are not wooden', can be read from the original, Diagram 4-10.

Furthermore, a simple diagram of 'All nonburnable things are not wooden' gives us the statement, 'All wooden things are burnable'. Examine Diagram 4-13, which represents 'All nonburnable things are not wooden'. Note that the space for wooden things (all that is outside the circle for non-

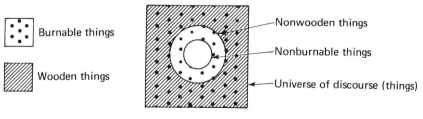

DIAGRAM 4-13

wooden things) is included in the space for burnable things (all that is outside the circle for nonburnable things). Hence the sentence, 'All wooden things are burnable', can be read from Diagram 4-13.

Since each of these sentences implies the other, they are logically equivalent. Either can be substituted for the other in an argument. Incidentally, it is interesting to note the similarity between this logical equivalence and that of contrapositives in sentence reasoning.

You should now see that if Example 4-4 had appeared in the following form we could have solved it with the same diagram as before, because we can substitute 'All wooden things can burn' for 'All nonburnable things are not wooden':

Example 4-8

All of the chairs in this room are wooden.
All nonburnable things are not wooden.

All of the chairs in this room can burn.

An alternative, of course, would be to leave the premises as they are and make a direct attack on the argument. This would put the circle for the chairs in this room outside the larger circle, because only nonwooden things are inside that larger circle. This placement requires that the circle for the chairs in this room also be outside the circle for nonburnable things, and thus be among the burnables. Thus the argument is again shown to be valid (Diagram 4-14). Sometimes it is more convenient to proceed one way, sometimes the other.

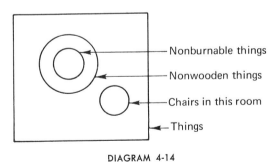

DIAGRAM 4-14

COMPREHENSION SELF-TEST

True or False? If the statement is false, change a crucial term (or terms) to make it true.

4-30. The universe of discourse is a larger class which includes all of the classes which play a role in the argument.

4–31. The universe of discourse is represented by a rectangle which appears around all circles.

4–32. 'All A's are B's' is logically the same as 'All non-A's are non-B's'.

Arguments to Diagram and Judge. Diagram each of the following arguments, labeling your diagram. Judge whether the argument is valid or invalid. In cases of invalidity make clear by means of alternate positions why you think the argument is invalid. In each case include a universe of discourse in your diagram.

4–33. Electric bells in complete circuits ring loudly. The front doorbell is in a complete circuit. Therefore, the front doorbell is ringing loudly.

4–34. Complementary colors are colors which when combined appear to be white. Blue and yellow are complementary colors. Therefore, blue and yellow when combined appear to be white.

4–35. Men who are not trusted by the American people are not elected president. Hence men who are elected president are trusted by the American people.

4–36. Bells in complete circuits ring loudly. The bell in my hand is not in a complete circuit. Hence it is not ringing loudly.

4–37. Men who are elected president by the American people are trusted by them. Blaine was not trusted by the American people. Hence he was not elected president.

4–38. Plants and animals which aren't closely related can't be crossed to produce hybrids. Since plants X and Y can be crossed to produce hybrids, they must be closely related.

4–39. People who know the proper rules of punctuation do well in their written compositions. Mary did not do well in her written compositions. Therefore, Mary does not know the proper rules of punctuation.

4–40. No true believers were heretics. All heretics were condemned. Therefore, no true believers were condemned.

4–41. ". . . none of woman born
Shall harm Macbeth."
". . . Macduff was from his mother's womb,
Untimely ripped."
Therefore, Macduff shall harm Macbeth.

Partial inclusion

The triangle example at the beginning of this chapter contained the key word 'some'. A seemingly obvious way to diagram sentences containing this word is to have overlapping circles, such as those of Diagram 4-15. Fundamentally this is a good idea, but precautions must be taken.

Ambiguity of 'some'

A major difficulty is that the word 'some' is used in two ways, 'at least some (and perhaps all)', and 'some, but not all'. In order to see this ambi-

guity, consider the sentence, 'Some of
the triangles on the page are inscribed
in semi-circles', and say it over to
yourself emphasizing different words.
The latter interpretation ('some, but
not all') is more common and should
ordinarily be the interpretation given,

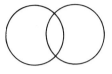

DIAGRAM 4-15

if there are no clues. If possible and if there is any doubt in your mind, you
should inquire about which is intended. Furthermore when **you** use the word,
if any doubt might arise in the minds of your audience, you should say either
'at least some' or 'some, but not all'.

'At least some'

Suppose we want to diagram the 'some' sentence which was one of the
premises in the triangle example, "At least some of the triangles on this
page are inscribed in semi-circles." This relationship is shown in Diagram
4-16. The dotted line indicates a boundary about which we are somewhat

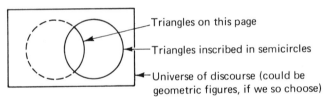

Triangles on this page

Triangles inscribed in semicircles

Universe of discourse (could be
geometric figures, if we so choose)

DIAGRAM 4-16

in doubt. There might be triangles on the page which are not inscribed in
semi-circles; there might not be such. This indeterminacy is indicated by
the dotted line. However, we do know from the premise that there are at
least some which **are** inscribed in semi-circles, and the solid part of the line,
which is inside the right-hand circle, so indicates.

Now we are in a position to diagram the triangle example (4-2) appearing
at the beginning of the chapter. You will remember that it goes like this:

All triangles inscribed in semi-circles are right triangles.
At least some of the triangles on this page are inscribed in semi-circles.

At least some of the triangles on this page are right triangles.

The validity of the argument is shown in Diagram 4-17. There is no way to
avoid putting at least a part of the circle for triangles on the page inside the
circle for right triangles. Hence the argument is shown to be valid.

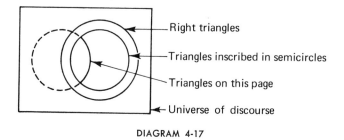

DIAGRAM 4-17

'Some, but not all'

Suppose that the previous 'some' sentence had been as follows:

Some, but not all of the triangles on this page are inscribed in semi-circles.

How should this be diagramed? Since the sentence tells us that there are triangles on this page which are not inscribed, we can diagram this by making the previous dotted line solid, as in Diagram 4-18. Part of the left-hand

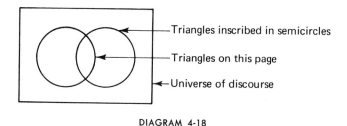

DIAGRAM 4-18

circle is definitely inside, and part is definitely outside the right-hand circle.

Consider the argument with the 'some-but-not-all' interpretation:

Example 4-9

All triangles inscribed in semi-circles are right triangles.
Some, but not all of the triangles on this page are inscribed in semi-circles.

Some, but not all of the triangles on this page are right triangles.

Is it valid? Diagram it and see.

Your diagram could look like that in Diagram 4-19. Since it was possible within the limits prescribed by the premises to put the whole circle for

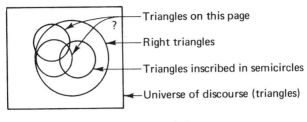

Triangles on this page

Right triangles

Triangles inscribed in semicircles

Universe of discourse (triangles)

DIAGRAM 4-19

triangles on this page inside the circle for right triangles, the argument is invalid. The conclusion, since it says "but not all", calls for the appearance of part of the area of the triangles-on-the-page circle outside the right-triangle circle. Since we were not inescapably forced to show that state of affairs in the diagram, the argument is invalid.

If this is not clear, it might help to think of the argument in symbolized form. Assume the following assignment of symbols:

Let '*A*'s' = 'triangles inscribed in semi-circles'
Let '*B*'s' = 'right triangles'
Let '*C*'s' = 'the triangles on this page'

Then the argument looks like this:

All *A*'s are *B*'s.
Some, but not all *C*'s are *A*'s.
––––––––––––––––––––––––––––
Some, but not all *C*'s are *B*'s.

From the premises we can see that it might well be that some, but not all *C*'s are *B*'s, but it could be the case that **all** the *C*'s are *B*'s. So the argument is invalid.

If, however, the conclusion were in terms of 'at least some', then the argument would again be valid. If this is not immediately clear to you, make a diagram and see that this is so.

Sometimes, when it is not clear which sense of 'some' is intended, you will find it profitable to diagram the argument several times, using the various possible interpretations. If you get the same result no matter what the interpretation, then you can be safe in making the judgment that it fits them all.

Partial exclusion

The word 'some' is used in negative sentences also. 'At least some *A*'s are not *B*'s' is diagramed as in Diagram 4-20. This diagram leaves open the possibility that at least some *A*'s are *B*'s.

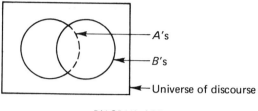

DIAGRAM 4-20

On the other hand, 'Some, but not all A's are not B's' is diagramed (Diagram 4-21) so that all of the circle for the A's is solid. This diagram tells

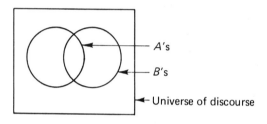

DIAGRAM 4-21

us that at least some A's are B's and that at least some A's are not B's. Since Diagram 4-21 is the same as a diagram for 'Some, but not all A's **are** B's', the two forms are logically equivalent.

COMPREHENSION SELF-TEST

True or False? If the statement is false, change a crucial term (or terms) to make it true.

4-42. The word 'some' is ordinarily to be interpreted as meaning 'at least some'.

4-43. A diagram for 'Some, but not all A's are B's' will have the circle for A's dotted in part.

4-44. A diagram for 'At least some A's are not B's' will have the circle for A's dotted in part.

Sentences to Diagram. Using a universe of discourse, diagram each of the following sentences, labeling the circles, and being careful about the placement of dotted lines.

4-45. At least some things that glitter are not gold.

4-46. Some of the poets in your text are romanticists.

4-47. Some bases are not strong.

4-48. At least some city governments are not corrupt.

4-49. At least some city governments are corrupt.

Arguments to Diagram and Judge. Diagram each of the following arguments, judging whether the argument is valid or invalid. In cases of invalidity, make clear by means of alternates why you think the argument is invalid.

4–50. Triangle *ABC* contains a right angle. Some triangles containing right angles are isosceles. Hence triangle *ABC* is isosceles.

4–51. The romanticists idealized life. Some of the poets in your text are romanticists. Therefore, some of the poets in your text idealized life.

4–52. All plants in which photosynthesis occurs need water. There are some plants, however, in which photosynthesis does not occur. Therefore, there are some plants which do not need water.

4–53. Some foods contain hydrogen and oxygen. All carbohydrates contain hydrogen and oxygen. Therefore, some foods are carbohydrates.

4–54. At least some things that glitter are not gold. The trinkets in this box glitter. Hence these trinkets are not gold.

4–55. At least some city governments are not corrupt. The government of New York, although complex, is still a city government. Hence it is not corrupt.

4–56. The liquid that I spilled on my lab table is a base. Since some bases are not strong, I can be sure that this liquid is not strong.

Multiple premises

This Euler circle system is useful for class reasoning arguments containing more than two premises. The thing to do is to look for premises with common classes and make use of the common classes to combine the premises in the same diagram. Again you work against the conclusion (but give it a chance, of course!). Here is a simple example using letters to stand for classes:

Example 4-10

All *A*'s are *B*'s.
All *B*'s are *C*'s.
All *C*'s are *D*'s.
_____
All *A*'s are *D*'s.

The diagram looks like Diagram 4-22. The conclusion is inescapably diagramed, so the argument is valid.

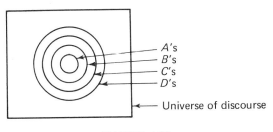

DIAGRAM 4-22

Here is a more difficult example, again using letters to stand for classes. It is more difficult because it requires a transformation on the side, which rates a separate diagram:

Example 4-11

All *D*'s are *B*'s.
All non-*D*'s are non-*C*'s.
All *B*'s are *A*'s.
_____

All *C*'s are *A*'s.

Try to work this yourself, before reading on.

One way to start is to transform the second premise so that it will have classes in common with the other premises. Perhaps you can do this in your head, but it is safer to put it on paper (Diagram 4-23). Since the area out-

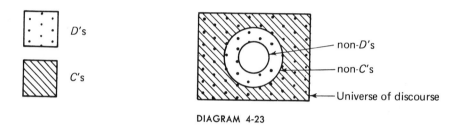

DIAGRAM 4-23

side the larger circle represents *C*'s, and the area outside the smaller circle represents *D*'s, we can say from this diagram that all *C*'s are *D*'s. If we substitute that for the second premise, then the problem becomes easy (Diagram 4-24). Since the conclusion is inescapably diagramed, the argument is valid.

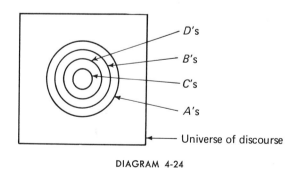

DIAGRAM 4-24

COMPREHENSION SELF-TEST

Arguments to Diagram and Judge. Diagram each of the following arguments, using a universe of discourse and labeling the circles with class terms. Judge whether the argument is valid, making clear by means of your diagram that the argument is as you judge it.

4–57. Any man who voted for Senator Smart has in effect voted against himself. John Brown voted for Senator Smart. It is obvious that anyone who votes against himself is a fool. Hence John Brown is a fool.

4–58. All genuine foods contain hydrogen and oxygen. This is also true of carbohydrates. Since all carbohydrates contain carbon, we can be sure that all genuine foods contain carbon.

4–59. Nobody who has attained historical fame has done it as a result of his own inherent greatness. All of the characters in the history book may be regarded as famous. Hence, Napoleon Bonaparte, a prominent figure in the history book, is not famous as a result of his own inherent greatness.

Note: The following arguments are a few of many similar arguments to be found in Lewis Carroll's book, *Symbolic Logic*, which was published under his real name, Charles Lutwidge Dodgson. Lewis Carroll was a mathematician and logician.

In these arguments, the conclusions are not given. You must figure out what conclusion follows necessarily and makes use of all the premises. Diagram the argument and write out the conclusion.

4–60. Babies are illogical. Nobody is despised who can manage a crocodile. Illogical persons are despised. What follows?

4–61. The only books in the library, that I do **not** recommend for reading, are unhealthy in tone. The bound books are all well written. All the romances are healthy in tone. I do not recommend you to read any of the unbound books. What follows?

4–62. No kitten, that loves fish, is unteachable. No kitten without a tail will play with a gorilla. Kittens with whiskers always love fish. No teachable kitten has green eyes. No kittens have tails unless they have whiskers.

4–63. No interesting poems are unpopular among people of real taste. No modern poetry is free from affectation. All your poems are on the subject of soap bubbles. No affected poetry is popular among people of real taste. No ancient poem is on the subject of soap bubbles. What follows?

Other interpretation problems

To express the thought behind the form, 'At least some *A*'s are not *B*'s', people frequently use a manner of speaking that strictly speaking means something else. They say, 'All that are *A*'s are not *B*'s.' For example in order to express the thought, 'At least some things that glitter are not gold', Shakespeare used the following: "All that glitters is not gold."

Strictly speaking, Shakespeare's form of words implies that everything that glitters is not gold. (If something glitters, then it is not gold.) Of course he did not mean this, so one must be careful in interpreting sentences that are of this form.

A little reflection will show you that another way of putting the same thought is in the form, 'Not all A's are B's.' In terms of the above example, the expression would be 'Not all that glitters is gold.' Diagram 4-25 repre-

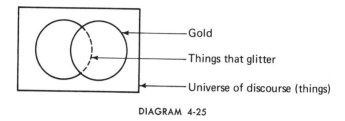

DIAGRAM 4-25

sents each of the two strict ways of expressing this thought. Examine it carefully. Each of the two sentences, 'At least some things that glitter are not gold' and 'Not all that glitters is gold' can be read from Diagram 4-25.

In traditional logic an elaborate system has been developed for determining the relationships between sentences like the above pair. Part of this system is referred to as "the square of opposition". The approach of this book is to depend upon the spatial relationships between circles, so I will not present the elaborate system, trusting that your grasp of the circle system will suffice. Some of you will find the elaborate system of interest and might consult some standard logic text for a treatment of it.* But an intelligent, cautious application of the Euler circle method should enable you to handle the practical problems for which the system can be of use.

No logical system has been organized which makes use of the distinctions in ordinary language that exist between 'few', 'much', 'several', 'many', 'most', etc. This Euler circle system is no exception. You must use common sense in applying this system to sentences containing such words.

Extent of the predicate class

So far we have ignored the ambiguity that is present in most of these sentences with respect to the predicate class. When we say that all A's are B's, that form of words does not tell whether there are B's which are not A's. It leaves open the possibility that there are B's which are not A's, but it also leaves open the possibility that there are no B's which are not A's.

* One standard text, which is as good as any other, is that by Morris Cohen and Ernest Nagel, *An Introduction to Logic and the Scientific Method* (New York: Harcourt, Brace and Company, 1934).

Hence from the form of the sentence, 'All A's are B's', we cannot conclude 'All B's are A's', nor can we conclude 'At least some B's are not A's'. Both possibilities are left open by the form of words, but neither is required.

Usually we can ignore this problem, but sometimes a judgment about an argument depends on our alertness to it. It is a good idea, when diagraming affirmative (as opposed to negative) statements, to remember that the extent of the predicate class is undetermined by the form of words. Sometimes it is determined by the context, and sometimes the extent does not matter. But be alert for this situation when working against the proposed conclusion.

Here is an example of an argument in which you might go wrong, if you are not alert for this situation:

Example 4-12

All right triangles can be inscribed in semi-circles.
All triangles in which the sum of two of the angles equals 90 degrees are right triangles.

At least some triangles which can be inscribed in semi-circles do not have the sum of two of their angles equal to 90 degrees.

A hasty diagram of that argument looks like Diagram 4-26. This diagram certainly suggests the conclusion, since some of the area for 'triangles that

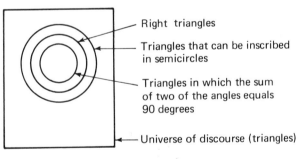

Right triangles

Triangles that can be inscribed in semicircles

Triangles in which the sum of two of the angles equals 90 degrees

Universe of discourse (triangles)

DIAGRAM 4-26

can be inscribed in semi-circles' is outside of the area for 'triangles in which the sum of two of the angles equals 90 degrees'. But to draw the proposed conclusion would be to depend on the assumption that the extent of the predicate class is greater than that of the subject class. This is an assumption which we never have a right to make on the basis of the form of the statements as they appear above, and which in this case is false for both premises.

Conclusions cannot depend on such an assumption unless it is explicitly part of the premises. When a statement of the form, 'All A's are B's', is made, we are left in doubt about whether at least some B's are not A's. That is,

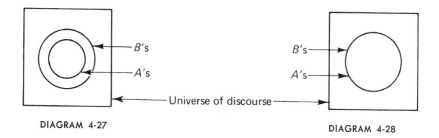

DIAGRAM 4-27   DIAGRAM 4-28

Diagrams 4-27 and 4-28 are left open as possibilities. In Diagram 4-27 the circle for the *A*'s is inside the circle for the *B*'s. In Diagram 4-28 the circles are the same size and in the same place. The two circles completely overlap, thus appearing as only one circle. This is the diagram that means that all *A*'s are *B*'s **and** all *B*'s are *A*'s. It is the possibility of this latter situation, as represented in Diagram 4-28, that makes it improper to make the above-mentioned assumption.

Taking the first premise of the example, Diagrams 4-29 and 4-30 are

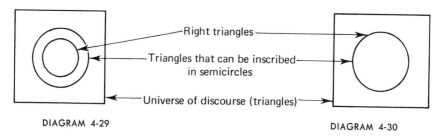

DIAGRAM 4-29   DIAGRAM 4-30

each a possibility, given only, "All right triangles can be inscribed in semi-circles." The same thing can be done with the second premise. In view of these alternatives for each premise, a possible way of diagraming the premises is shown in Diagram 4-31, which does not force us to accept the conclusion. Hence the argument is invalid.

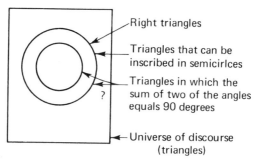

DIAGRAM 4-31

This way of working against the conclusion of an argument illustrates the fact that this system is only an aid to your judgment in dealing with arguments. It is not a strictly mechanical system, but must be used with care and ingenuity.

COMPREHENSION SELF-TEST

True or False? If the statement is false, change a crucial term (or terms) to make it true.

4-64. The Euler circle system which you have learned does not make a distinction between 'a few' and 'several'.

4-65. The use of the form, 'All *A*'s are *B*'s', implies that there are *B*'s which are not *A*'s.

4-66. Strictly speaking, 'All of the lake doesn't have fish' means that there are no fish in the lake.

Arguments to Diagram and Judge. Diagram and label each of the following arguments, using a universe of discourse. Judge the validity, making clear why you judge as you do.

4-67. Every bishop was an important church official. Many important church officials held fiefs from kings. Therefore, many bishops held fiefs from kings.

4-68. Some fiefs were held by secular lords. Many fiefs held by secular lords were hereditary. Hence some fiefs were hereditary.

4-69. Not all rhombuses are similar. *A* and *B* are two polygons that are not similar. Therefore *A* and *B* are rhombuses.

4-70. People who spell English words exactly as they sound misspell some of them. Joe misspells many English words. Therefore, Joe spells many English words exactly as they sound.

4-71. All that glitters is not gold. This case glitters. Hence it is not gold.

4-72. All of the members of the team did not break training. Only if everyone on the team broke training will we lose. Hence we will not lose. (Note: Use whatever procedures seem appropriate for this argument.)

4-73. The buildings on the campus are all of Gothic architecture. Whatever is of Gothic architecture is out of step with the times. Hence the buildings on the campus are out of step with the times, and there are things which are out of step with the times which are not on this campus.

4-74. Whatever is in the animal kingdom is not in the plant kingdom. Lobsters are in the plant kingdom. Hence there are things not in the plant kingdom which are not lobsters.

Combination of Class and Sentence Reasoning

Contemporary logic contains a system—with many variations—which combines sentence and class reasoning by elaborating sentence reasoning and introducing a more complicated symbolism. The resulting system for handling class reasoning is often called the "predicate calculus". I do not believe that one need master this system in order to handle problems in everyday reasoning, although the system is interesting in its own right and is valuable in understanding the foundations of mathematics and some of contemporary philosophy.

Part-by-part use of the two systems

You can use in combination the two systems when faced with arguments that involve both class and sentence reasoning. You might treat the diagrams as sentences which can be joined by the logical connectives you have studied. Or you might be able to work the parts separately in the different systems. For example consider this argument, again about Ingrid's dough:

Example 4-13
Only if Ingrid's dough contains yeast mixed with lukewarm water did she make the check in her book. Now we know that dough containing yeast mixed with lukewarm water rises rapidly. And we also know that she made the check in her book. Hence we know that her dough is rising rapidly.

An examination of this argument shows that, using the techniques of sentence reasoning, we can combine the first and the third sentences to produce the subconclusion, "Ingrid's dough contains yeast mixed with lukewarm water." Using the techniques of class reasoning we can combine this subconclusion with the second sentence to produce the given conclusion. I shall work it out in detail:

Example 4-14
Let 'q' = 'Ingrid's dough contains yeast mixed with lukewarm water'
Let 'p' = 'she made the check in her book'

Premises (of the sentence reasoning part of the argument):

$p \longrightarrow q$
p

Conclusion (of this part of the argument):

q (by affirmation of the antecedent)

So far we are entitled to conclude that Ingrid's dough contains yeast mixed with lukewarm water. Examination of Diagram 4-32 shows the rest of the argument, and thus the total argument, to be valid.

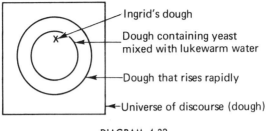

Ingrid's dough

Dough containing yeast
mixed with lukewarm water

Dough that rises rapidly

Universe of discourse (dough)

DIAGRAM 4-32

Instantiation

You will remember that one of the occasions for the introduction of the Euler circle system was in part the inability of strictly interpreted sentence reasoning to handle Example 4-1, which went as follows:

Dough containing yeast mixed with lukewarm water rises rapidly.
Ingrid's dough contains yeast mixed with lukewarm water.

Therefore Ingrid's dough rises rapidly.

The problem was that a transformation of the first premise to conditional form did not produce two separate affirmable sentences:

If any dough contains yeast mixed with lukewarm water, then that dough rises rapidly.

To say "Ingrid's dough contains yeast mixed with lukewarm water" is not to say "Any dough contains yeast mixed with lukewarm water", the latter of these looking something, but not quite, like an antecedent of the conditional, and not being meaningfully affirmable.

In contemporary logic a useful move has been developed for this kind of situation. I will describe it because it is sometimes more convenient to use this move than to use the Euler circle system, depending mainly on the form in which the premise happens to be naturally stated. This move is called instantiation. The following step from the more general to more specific statement is an example of instantiation:

Example 4-15

FROM:
    If any dough contains yeast mixed with lukewarm water, than that dough rises rapidly.
TO:
    If Ingrid's dough contains yeast mixed with lukewarm water, then Ingrid's dough will rise rapidly.

In effect the specific reference to Ingrid's dough was substituted for the variable reference to any dough. Note that we can affirm the new antecedent without uttering nonsense; thus the result of the instantiation step is suitable for use in sentence reasoning.

To INSTANTIATE a conditional statement is to give its application to a specific situation, the result being another (but specific) conditional. The move is an intuitively plausible one and removes the barrier to treating a number of deductions in sentence reasoning terms. Once we have made the move in the dough example, we can take the instantiation and use it as a premise as follows:

Example 4-16
If Ingrid's dough contains yeast mixed with lukewarm water, then Ingrid's dough will rise rapidly.
Ingrid's dough contains yeast mixed with lukewarm water.

Ingrid's dough will rise rapidly.
Valid. Affirming the antecedent.

Whether you actually choose to use instantiation or the circle method in any particular case is partly a matter of taste and partly a matter of convenience.

Ingenuity is often required in devising ways to judge arguments, but with an understanding of the ways of handling arguments presented in this and the previous chapter, you should be able to work out any long deductive reasoning problems that you will genuinely face. Generally, long arguments become simple by being broken up into parts that can be managed with the basic techniques you have seen.

COMPREHENSION SELF-TEST

Arguments to Judge. Here is a set of arguments. Using any techniques that you feel are appropriate, decide whether each argument is valid. But show all your work.

4-75. Either the present municipal airport should continue to be used for purposes of general aviation, or it should be used to provide a site for a summer festival every year, but not both. It should continue to be used for general aviation only if the other airport is to be closed down. The other airport is not to be closed down; rather it is to be expanded. Hence the municipal airport should be used to provide a site for a summer festival each year.

4-76. If Brown has a position on the Rules Committee, then all the men on this list have declined to serve. Jones is on the list, and he has declined to serve only if he was appointed to the Appropriations Committee. Since Jones was not appointed to this last-named committee, Brown has not secured a position on the Rules Committee.

4-77. Only if the piece of wood sinks in the beaker of alcohol is its specific gravity greater than one. Anything with a specific gravity greater than one will sink in water. The piece of wood sinks in alcohol. Hence it will sink in water.

4-78. Most household chemicals are safe to touch. If any chemical is not safe to touch, however, then it is so labeled. There is no label indicating danger on this bottle of citric acid. Therefore, it is safe to touch.

4-79. All of Beethoven's works are solid and deliberate. Now Frank does not like music that is solid and deliberate, and whatever he does not like he does not really listen to. He is really listening to this music only if his eyes are closed. Since his eyes are not closed, we can conclude two things: (1) Frank does not like this piece, and (2) it is by Beethoven.

4-80. All well-lighted rooms have light-colored walls. Some of the rooms in Stone Hall are small. All of the rooms in Stone Hall either have very dark-colored walls, or have no windows, or are large, or are well lighted. The rooms in Stone Hall that are not well lighted are on the east side. All of the rooms on the east side have windows. If some of the rooms in Stone Hall are small, then my room in Stone Hall is small. The walls in my room are not light colored. Therefore, the walls in my room are very dark in color.

Chapter Summary

In the system presented in this chapter, a modified Euler circle system, the classes and individuals which are the basic units in class reasoning are, for purposes of seeing relationships, represented by circles and the letter 'x'. Often, however, sentences as they appear must be revised in order to bring out the class relationships to be put in a circle diagram. This revision most often requires that the predicate of the sentence be changed to contain a class, which is connected to the subject by the verb of inclusion (or membership), the verb, 'to be'. For example the sentence, 'This tree grows quickly', becomes 'This tree is a quickly growing thing' or 'This tree is a quick grower'.

When this sort of revision, if necessary, is accomplished, the classes are represented on paper in the form of circles. The inclusion of one class in another is represented by the inclusion of one circle in the other. The membership of one individual in a class is represented by the appearance of an 'x' to represent the individual in the circle to represent the class.

Exclusion is represented by keeping these things separate from each other. Partial inclusion is shown by partial overlapping (with dotted lines to show where boundaries are uncertain), and partial exclusion is shown by partially separate circles (again using dotted lines to show boundaries that are uncertain).

Since a standard class inclusion statement of the form, 'All A's are B's', does not indicate whether there are B's which are not A's, one must remember that the extent of the circle for the predicate class is in doubt. That it occupies the same place as that for the subject class is not ruled out by the form, 'All A's are B's'.

One determines whether an argument is valid by putting the premises into one diagram, combining them where possible. In so doing one tries not to diagram the proposed conclusion, doing justice of course to the premises. If the conclusion is inescapably diagramed by the diagraming of the premises, then the argument is valid.

Combinations of class and sentence reasoning can be handled by breaking the argument into component parts and treating each part appropriately. In such combinations, as with all genuine arguments, one must use care and common sense, since the systems offered are not simply automatic. No realistic logic can be.

Instantiation, which is basically a class reasoning step, can be used to accommodate the methods of sentence reasoning to some deductions which appear in class reasoning form. In many cases the choice between the circle system and sentence reasoning (with instantiation) is a matter of taste and convenience.

CHAPTER 5

Practical Application
of Deductive Logic

Perhaps you have already noticed that when you actually apply the techniques and rules of deductive reasoning presented in the previous three chapters, you run into snags. The snags are generally of two types: those resulting from the fact that much deductive-like reasoning occurs which does not strictly conform to the principles of ideal deduction; and those resulting from the fact that there are other forms of necessary inference than the ones you have studied here. This chapter treats those two types of snags.

Looseness of Reasoning

The term, 'looseness', as it appears in this chapter, is not meant to be a pejorative term. It is used simply to show recognition of the facts of life: the standards of deduction cannot be applied strictly and directly to many cases of actual reasoning that go from general statements to specific ones and appear deductive in form. This is a strong statement, the truth of which becomes evident when one tries to take these standards seriously and tries to apply them directly to respectable inference practice in most fields of study.

In what follows, I shall develop a model which makes reasonable use of deductive standards, and consider then a number of examples drawn from different fields in order to show how this model can be applied. Please realize that this problem of looseness is not one to which logicians have devoted much attention. The solution to it, even among those who recognize that it exists, has not been a subject of intense, disciplined, comprehensive treatment. Hence you should not treat what you are about to read as doctrine received and accepted by the philosophical community. Instead look at it as something placed before you in an attempt to make sense out of what is otherwise a puzzling situation.

Actually the proposed model is not at all complicated. It simply treats strict deduction as an idealized set of inference patterns to which we shift in judging the formal moves in an argument. Thus there are basically three steps in this model: (1) the shift into idealized form; (2) the judgment of the validity of the idealized form thus produced; and (3) the shift from the idealized conclusion back to the world of reality. In actual practice these three steps are not sharply distinguished. Generally one merges the three together. They are separated here so that a role for strict deduction can become explicit, and so that deviations from the strict deductive pattern can be explained.

Step 1 : the shift into idealized form

In this first step the premises are put into shape, partly by revision to fit some recognizable formal pattern, and partly by eliminating implicit and explicit general qualifiers. By 'GENERAL QUALIFIERS' I mean such terms as 'probably', 'likely', 'generally', 'for the most part', 'under normal conditions', 'ceteris paribus' ('other things being equal'),* 'by and large', and 'roughly speaking'. These are general because they are not limited to any subject matter or branch of inquiry.

Implicit qualifications are eliminated by simply ignoring them. Explicit qualifications are eliminated by dropping them off for the purposes of Step 2. Consider this statement:

Example 5-1
A wind shift from south to northwest is generally accompanied by clearing and colder weather.

---

* ❖It is somewhat of a simplification to group 'under normal conditions' and 'other things being equal' with the rest, but the simplification does not damage the general approach recommended here, so long as one keeps the meaning of the eliminated qualifier in mind. An alternative system suggested by Professor David Lyons would allow the retention of these two qualifiers in the general statements of the premises and for the deduction test in Step 2 would add a presumably implicit premise affirming the satisfaction of the qualifier. Then the problems discussed later under Step 3 must in part be faced when deciding whether and how strongly to endorse the implicit premise.

Deletion of the term 'generally' would effect the transformation into idealized form.

Example 5-2
Other things being equal, if the demand for a commodity decreases, the price will decrease (assuming that the supply remains the same).

In this last example deletion of 'other things being equal' effects the transformation. Note, however, that one specific condition is singled out for the requirement that it be equal (remain the same): the supply. Mention of this specific condition is not to be deleted in the transformation. The only qualifiers that are deleted are the general qualifiers. The qualifier, "the supply remains the same", is specific to the subject matter of the principle.

Example 5-3
Each one of the periods of lax financial integrity coincides with periods when a new set of frontier communities had arisen, and coincides in area with these successive frontiers, for the most part.*

Deletion of the phrase, 'for the most part', would transform this general statement into idealized form, if the phrase qualifies the entire statement. If it only qualifies coincidence in area, then we need only delete it for certain purposes. We will go into this later.

In this next example there are no explicit general qualifiers.

Example 5-4
English literature of the first fifty years of the eighteenth century was neoclassical.

However, anyone at all versed in the field of literature knows that there are always exceptions to such statements, which fact could be shown by the use of the qualifier 'generally'. But the existence of such exceptions apparently is such common knowledge that people take it for granted and do not bother to insert explicit qualifiers, leaving them implicit. Hence elimination of the qualifiers in such cases simply consists in temporarily forgetting the common knowledge that there are exceptions.

Step 1 also includes whatever else is needed to put the premises in shape for the application of techniques presented in the previous three chapters. Although no precise line can be drawn between putting the premises in shape and using deductive techniques,** there still is a distinction between

---

* Frederick Jackson Turner, "The Significance of the Frontier in American History," a paper read at the meeting of the American Historical Association in Chicago, July 12, 1893, and reprinted in various places, including Turner's *The Frontier in American History* (New York: Henry Holt and Company, 1921), p. 32.

** "Putting an Argument in Shape" (see Chapter 3) was one of the headings in the material dealing with deductive techniques.

the preliminary procedures requiring intelligent judgment and the application of rule-governed techniques.

Step 2 : judgment of validity

This step was the subject of the previous three chapters. An explicit validity test must be applied. Consider this simple example:

Example 5-5
Premises:
A wind shift from south to northwest is accompanied by clearing and colder weather.
The wind shift that just occurred was a shift from south to northwest.
Conclusion:
The wind shift that just occurred will be accompanied by clearing and colder weather.*

The argument is valid, as can be seen by an inspection of Diagram 5-1.

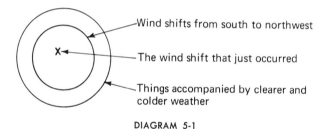

Wind shifts from south to northwest

The wind shift that just occurred

Things accompanied by clearer and colder weather

DIAGRAM 5-1

In order to adjust the first premise and conclusion to the diagram system, they were put in the form of class relationship statements.

A wind shift from south to northwest is a thing accompanied by clearing and colder weather.
The wind shift that just occurred will be a thing accompanied by clearing and colder weather.

The explicit validity test that was applied was the rule about trying to avoid diagraming the conclusion.

Step 3 : the shift from the conclusion back to the world of reality

This step is the most risky and difficult one. No set procedures exist for weakening the conclusion and/or deciding whether it should be asserted.

---

* For purposes of simplicity I shall ignore the tense differences in the verbs here. In some cases such shifts do make a difference, so be wary.

This step requires a familiarity with the field in which the subject matter is located and experience in drawing conclusions in this field. It also depends on the context. Since there are no explicit exceptionless rules to follow, one can expect that experts in the given field will in some cases disagree on the results. This part of practical reasoning is an art which calls for the intelligent exercise of experienced judgment.

In the weather-prediction example the appropriate conclusion might well be the following:

Example 5-6
The wind shift that just occurred will probably be accompanied by clearing and
colder weather.

The word 'probably' has been inserted, because the science of weather prediction calls for some sort of indication that the prediction might not be fulfilled. This word 'probably' performs the function of letting one's audience know that the asserter, although reasonably confident of his statement, does not want to guarantee it unconditionally. He explicitly disclaims full endorsement of the statement. In this case, if you were the person making the weather prediction, you would by the use of 'probably' be explicitly disclaiming full endorsement of the statement that the wind shift that just occurred will be accompanied by clearing and colder weather.* A variety of considerations can justify this disclaimer.

For example the premises might not be indentical with true factual reports, perhaps because the premises are more vague or more specific. Suppose in trying to decide whether to apply the generalization in Example 5-1, one learns that the wind was from 190 degrees (180 degrees is due south) and has shifted to being from 300 degrees (exactly northwest is 315 degrees). Has there been a shift from south to northwest? Answering this question requires familiarity with the field. Inevitably there will be borderline cases and disagreement among experts. In this case I presume that most would say that there has been such a shift and that the generalization would still apply. But in any case intelligent, informed, experienced judgment is needed.

Rejection. Furthermore under certain conditions one might justifiably decide that the conclusion, even with the word 'probably' inserted, should not be asserted. The ability to make decisions of this sort calls for expertise, familiarity, and experience. In the weather-prediction example, if the wind shift is the result of a local thunderstorm that develops in advance of a warm front, then it probably will not be accompanied by clearing and colder. Furthermore it will probably soon be followed by a wind shift back to the

---

* The use of the word 'probably' and terms like it is discussed in J. O. Urmson's "Parenthetical Verbs," in Antony Flew, ed., *Essays in Conceptual Analysis* (London: Macmillan & Co. Ltd., 1956), pp. 192–212; and in S. Toulmin's article, "Probability," in the same volume, pp. 157–91.

south. There are other standard exceptions as well, but mention of this one makes the point.

Uncertainty. A similar problem exists in the application of the generalization in a different type of surrounding, say Death Valley, California, or Vienna, or Tibet, or Mars. Again experience and expertise is required in deciding whether the conclusion should be asserted, even with the word 'probably' included.

Application to the Situation. In the process of applying the conclusions of practical reasoning, the problem of vagueness reappears. In order to avoid being paralyzed by a degree of imprecision in our knowledge, and/or in order to avoid unnecessary precision, we make use of ways of saying things that are to an extent vague. This leads to borderline cases and indeterminacy. Consider Example 5-6. Suppose that one wants to know whether to make plans for an airplane take-off in exactly one hour. The given conclusion does not tell one exactly when to expect the accompanying clearing. Suppose that one wants to know whether a pond will freeze overnight. The given conclusion does not specify how much colder it will be. Actually our meteorological knowledge warrants more precision than that given in the prediction of Example 5-6, but a more complicated principle must be used than the one given as the first premise in the argument, and more facts must be used as other premises.

This sort of vagueness is also a problem when dispute arises about the truth of the generalization: Someone offers as counter-evidence to the generalization the fact that it is one hour after the wind shift, but the weather actually looks more ominous and there has been a temperature drop of only one degree. Is this counter-evidence or not? Again intelligent informed judgment is required.

The Broader Logical Context. This last-described situation brings to mind another factor to which one must attend: the broader logical move in which the argument plays a role. Four such broader moves which frequently occur are prediction, retrodiction, explanation, and hypothesis-testing.

The weather case, as discussed, exemplifies prediction, and shows some of the sorts of considerations which bear upon the expressed degree of endorsement of the conclusion. Retrodiction is similar to prediction, except that retrodiction applies to the past, while prediction applies to the future. When we conclude that a certain thing probably happened and make use of reasoning processes similar to those used in prediction, we are RETRODICTING. For example suppose that we know that five days ago, when the weather was bad, the wind shifted from south to northwest. We might on this basis make the following retrodiction: The weather probably cleared up soon thereafter. And again judicious use of experience and theoretical knowledge should temper our use of 'probably'—or our complete rejection of the retrodiction.

Arguments also play a role in some kinds of explanation. If we want to explain why the weather cleared during the day, we might point out the fact that the wind shifted early this morning, and, making use of the generalization, show that the thing to be explained follows loosely from the fact and the generalization. In this case the deduction is not used to show that its conclusion is true, for we already know that it is true. What we want is an explanation of why it is true—and, given an appropriate context, this explanation is provided by the deductive argument leading to the conclusion. In this sort of situation it does not make sense to add such words as 'probably' to the conclusion, because we already know it to be true. The word 'probably' would imply that we do not **know** that the conclusion is true, but merely have good reason to believe it to be true.

Deductive arguments also play a role in the testing of hypotheses. The role is a complicated one, but let me point out here that the implications of a hypothesis often count as tests of the hypothesis. Roughly speaking if an implication turns out to be false, then by denial of the consequent, the hypothesis is thereby shown to be false (unless one of the assumptions is abandoned). And if the implications turn out to be true, then under certain conditions, the hypothesis thereby achieves a greater degree of credibility. Of course, each of these results is subject to experience and theoretical knowledge.

Granting the above brief analysis of the relation between a hypothesis and its implications, and construing the hypothesis as one of the premises in an argument and an implication as the conclusion to an argument, we then face the question of how strongly to endorse such a conclusion. In the case in which the hypothesis is something about which we are not sure, and we have not yet checked to see if the implication (the conclusion) is true, we are not in a position to endorse the conclusion, but neither are we in a position to deny it. Hence we must say something like this: "The hypothesis makes the conclusion probable", hedging against direct endorsement and denial, and instead only indicating degree of endorsement of the argument from hypothesis to implication.

These comments about prediction, retrodiction, explanation, and hypothesis are not meant to cover comprehensively all types of situations. Instead they are intended to note some significant differences in some common broad logical moves in which arguments play a role, and to suggest ways in which we attend to these differences in phrasing and endorsing conclusions to arguments.

False Premises and Invalid Arguments. You will remember from the discussion in Chapter 2 that one can have a true conclusion to a valid argument, even though the premises are false. Furthermore, it is also possible to have a true conclusion to an invalid argument utilizing true premises. And lastly one can have a true conclusion to an invalid argument containing false premises. Thus these defects in argument and/or premises do not by themselves justify rejection of the conclusion; but they do show that the conclusion is not established by the argument.

Summary

The three steps (shift to idealized form, judgment of validity, and shift from the conclusion back to the world of reality), which are treated separately for purposes of examining the problems of practical reasoning, are performed in concert in actual cases of reasoning. Furthermore, although Step 2, the application of deductive techniques, can be at times fairly difficult, it is generally the easiest step; the other two require careful, intelligent, informed judgment, which for its background and degree of specificity must depend on the context, the nature of the subject matter involved, and the knowledge of it that we possess.

Other Types of Deduction

Not all deductive arguments, even after the appropriate adjustments for looseness have been made, can be judged by the criteria given for sentence and class reasoning. There are other types of deduction. To some extent an understanding of sentence and class reasoning is helpful in dealing with other types, because one who does understand these two has a grasp of the basic idea of necessary inference and because in some cases the techniques for sentence and class reasoning loosely apply to others. For example the transitivity of the conditional chain is paralleled by the transitivity of equality and of ordinal relationships:

If $p \longrightarrow q$ and $q \longrightarrow r$, then $p \longrightarrow r$
  is parallel to
If $x = y$ and $y = z$, then $x = z$
  and also to
If n is greater than m and m is greater k, then n is greater than k.

In order to give warning of the types of problems that one might face, I shall describe briefly some other types of deduction. Since no successful comprehensive classification of types of deduction has to my knowledge ever been prepared, I make no claim about the comprehensiveness of this list.

Mathematics

A wide variety of deductive techniques are used in mathematical proofs: reduction of fractions, derivation of formulas, manipulating and solving equations, and many other techniques. These are deductive because, given the premises, the conclusion necessarily follows. The deductive relationship holds not only for complex mathematical proofs, but also for the very simple relationships one learns to use in his early years of schooling. This book makes no attempt to present the deductive techniques of mathematics.

Alethic logic*

This is the logic of the relationship between possibilities. A rule in this sort of logic might be the following:

If p is a necessary truth, and if p implies q, then q is a necessary truth.

Deontic logic*

This is the logic of obligation statements. A possible rule is this one:

If you are obligated to do x, and if you cannot do x without doing y, then you are obligated to do y, unless there is good reason not to do y.

Epistemic logic*

This is the logic of relationships between knowledge, beliefs, and claims about the truth. Here is a possible rule:

If someone knows that p is true, then p is true.

Spatial logic

This is the logic of spatial relationships. On it is based the model used for class reasoning in Chapter 4, the Euler circle model. Here is a rule:

If a given area, A, is inside an area, B, and if the area, B, is inside an area, C, then the area, A, is inside the area, C.

Other types

Other types of deductive logic also exist, often in such unorganized form that no name has been suggested for them. For example, relationships between claims about what is good and what a person ought to do are possible rules of inference in some type of deductive logic. But in any case, systems of alethic, deontic, epistemic, and others yet unnamed are generally quite controversial. Much work needs to be done before they attain the less

---

* The terms, 'alethic', 'deontic', and 'epistemic' are used by G. H. von Wright, in his attempt to categorize some types of logic. See his *Logical Studies* (London: Routledge & Kegan Paul Ltd., 1957), pp. 58–74.

controversial state of sentence reasoning, class reasoning, spatial reasoning, and mathematical reasoning.

Examples of Practical Reasoning in More Detail

A look at several more examples of practical reasoning might be instructive. In developing these examples, I have consulted experts in the fields involved. This act of consultation fits in with the view expressed: that proper performance of practical reasoning requires familiarity and experience with the subject matter involved. This consultation, however, did not result in sophisticated examples that can be understood only by one versed in the field. Rather they are intentionally fairly simple so that all of them can be understood by the nonexpert. All have many more complications than will be introduced, but that is due to the nature of practical reasoning: it is not the simple, elegant thing that one hopes to find after studying pure deduction.

An aspect of the frontier thesis

Frederick Jackson Turner, an American historian who lived from 1861 to 1932, offered in 1893 the suggestion to his fellow historians that they look more closely at the frontier conditions of American life in their attempts to explain and understand events and trends in American history. One statement that he made concerned "periods of lax financial integrity" and was quoted earlier (Example 5-3) as one illustration of the use of explicit qualifiers ("for the most part"). Here is the first stage of an argument constructed on the basis of his general statement:

Example 5-7
Premises:*
P-1: Each one of these periods of lax financial integrity coincides with periods when a new set of frontier communities had arisen, and coincides in area with these successive frontiers, for the most part.
P-2: There was a great deal of lax financial integrity in the period prior to the crisis of 1837.
Conclusion:
C-1: The period prior to the crisis of 1837 coincides with the period of a new set of frontier communities.

Conclusion 1 does not take us very far, but for the time being let us concentrate only on the reasoning leading up to it. In a real situation this con-

---

* In order to facilitate reference to the parts of arguments, labeling systems are here adopted which are more extensive than those used in the main part of Chapter 3. Different systems are used in order to illustrate a flexibility of labeling to fit a situation.

clusion could be derived in an attempt to make a retrodiction (like a prediction, but about the past) based upon Turner's claim and serving as a test of the claim. Admittedly it would not be a very good test, because the phrase, "period of a new set of frontier communities", is vague, and because there were almost continuously new sets of frontier communities. Alternatively the conclusion could be derived in an attempt to show that Turner's claim explains the occurrence of some events around 1837. Such explanatory power is often offered as evidence in support of a hypothesis.

Step 1. The Shift into Idealized Form. In my opinion the qualification, "for the most part", only qualifies the coincidence in area and is not a qualification of the entire statement. We can then use deductive techniques leading to Conclusion 1 without removing the qualification; hence it need not be removed. But we will need to ignore the ever-present implicit qualification to generalizations in history while we use our deductive techniques. Some revision though is required in the first premise, because strictly speaking it is absurd. It sets periods of time in coincidence with areas in the second major clause:

> Each one of these **periods** of lax financial integrity . . . coincides in **area** with these successive frontiers, for the most part. [Emphasis added]

Presumably Turner meant the entire sentence to mean the following:

> Each one of these periods of lax financial integrity coincides with a period* when a new set of frontier communities had arisen, and the area of the lax financial integrity coincides with that of these successive frontiers, for the most part.

Now we have periods coinciding with periods and areas coinciding with areas. Although this revision is not needed for the derivation of Conclusion 1 it is probably best to set things straight from the beginning.

The second premise also requires some revision. It looks like this:

> There was a great deal of lax financial integrity in the period prior to the crisis of 1837.

I would revise it as follows:

> The period prior to the crisis of 1837 was a period of lax financial integrity.

This revision is made with the general premise in mind. The revision enables one to put the two premises together to produce a conclusion, because there is a common class, *periods of lax financial integrity.*

---

* A minor change here from plural to singular. Presumably he would have one period coincide with another, instead of a set of them.

Step 2: Judgment of Validity. The argument, reproduced below as revised, is valid, as can be seen by an inspection of the diagram.

Example 5-8

Premises:

P–1: Each one of these periods of lax financial integrity coincides with a period when a new set of frontier communities had arisen, and the area of the lax financial integrity coincides with that of these successive frontiers, for the most part.

P–2: The period prior to the crisis of 1837 was a period of lax financial integrity.

Conclusion:

C–1: The period prior to the crisis of 1837 coincides with a period of a new set of frontier communities.

Using only that part of the first premise which precedes the first comma, we have Diagram 5-2. The argument is valid.

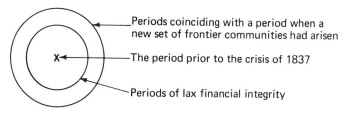

DIAGRAM 5-2

Step 3. The Shift from the Conclusion back to the World of Reality. Should the word 'probably' be inserted in the conclusion to this valid argument? That depends in part on the context. If the purpose of the argument is to generate a retrodiction, on which one might base future decisions (about what to look for, what to expect to find, etc.), then we would insert the word 'probably' (assuming Turner's general claim to be true):

> The period prior to the crisis of 1837 probably coincided with a period of a new set of frontier communities.

If, on the other hand, we know that there was a coincidence of two such periods, and are trying to explain this coincidence, then we do not insert 'probably'. If one knows that there was a coincidence, then it is misleading for him to say that there probably was a coincidence.

Remember though that this first conclusion, because of its vagueness and the frequent presence of periods of new frontier communities, is not very informative. But it is a step toward a conclusion that is more informative. Let us turn to the development of this informative conclusion.

Suppose we know that, as retrodicted (or explained), the conclusion is true in virtue of the fact that there actually was a period of new frontier communities prior to the period of the crisis of 1837, and that Cincinnati, Ohio, is one of the communities typically mentioned as a frontier community at that time. Naturally there will be some hesitation about this piece of knowledge because of the vagueness of Turner's usage of the word 'period'. But suppose that we, relying on our experience and understanding of the field of American history, judge this to be a piece of knowledge. The coincidence of the period of new communities (including Cincinnati) with the period prior to the crisis (using 'period' fairly loosely) convinces us that the conclusion to the previous argument is true. Then we can go on to make new retrodictions—or to explain other alleged facts: that the area in which lax financial integrity was to be found coincides for the most part with the new frontier area—and more particularly that probably lax financial integrity existed in Cincinnati at the time.

Look at the total argument in which everything we know is put into the premises and in which two conclusions are generated, the broad one and the particular one about Cincinnati:

Example 5-9

Premises:

P-1: Each one of these periods of lax financial integrity coincides with periods when a new set of frontier communities had arisen, and coincides in area with these successive frontiers, for the most part.

P-2: There was a great deal of lax financial integrity in the period prior to the crisis of 1837.

P-3: Cincinnati was in the area of the frontier of the period prior to the crisis of 1837.

Conclusions:

C-2: The area of these new frontier communities prior to the time of the crisis of 1837 was for the most part characterized by lax financial integrity.

C-3: Cincinnati probably was characterized by lax financial integrity.

Step 1. What needs to be done? The first two premises need the revisions indicated earlier (Example 5-8). In addition the qualifier, 'for the most part', must be dropped from the first premise. Lastly the phrase 'these successive frontiers' should be changed to 'the frontier area of the time'. This is because we are now going to use only the second part of the first premise and will be thrown off by reference to the first part. The meaning is not changed.

In order to fit a valid form of argument (and one must look ahead to Step 2 to know this), the conclusions must be reworded as well:

C-2: The area of lax financial integrity of the period prior to the crisis of 1837 coincides with the area of the frontier of the time.

C-3: Cincinnati was in an area of lax financial integrity.

The use of Conclusion 1 is now apparent. It is a presupposition to Conclusion 2; the latter would not make sense if there were no "frontier area of the time".

Next, just to be sure that all is clear, I shall rewrite the premises and conclusions in accord with changes just indicated:

Example 5-10

Premises:

P–1: Each one of these periods of lax financial integrity coincides with a period when a new set of frontier communities had arisen, and the area of the lax financial integrity coincides with that of the frontier area of the time.

P–2: The period prior to the crisis of 1837 was a period of lax financial integrity.

P–3: Cincinnati was in the area of the frontier of the period prior to the crisis of 1837.

Conclusions:

C–2: The area of lax financial integrity of the period of the crisis of 1837 coincided with the area of the frontier of the time.

C–3: Cincinnati was in an area of lax financial integrity.

Step 2. Examination of Diagram 5-3 shows the argument for the second

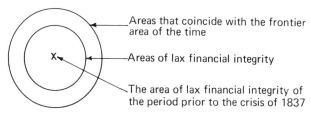

Areas that coincide with the frontier area of the time

Areas of lax financial integrity

The area of lax financial integrity of the period prior to the crisis of 1837

DIAGRAM 5-3

conclusion to be valid. We now can use the second conclusion as a premise to derive the third conclusion. It becomes P-4 in the following argument:

Example 5-11

Premises:

P–3: Cincinnati was in the area of the frontier of the period prior to the crisis of 1837.

P–4: The area of lax financial integrity of the period prior to the crisis of 1837 coincided with the frontier area of the time.

Conclusion:

C–3: Cincinnati was in an area of lax financial integrity.

To show the validity of this argument we first use spatial reasoning, a technique analogous to that developed in class reasoning. You will remember that spatial reasoning includes the basic technique of inclusion of areas on which the Euler circle system is based. We use a circle to represent the geographical area of lax financial integrity of the period prior to the 1837 crisis. According to the fourth premise (which is also the second conclusion), this area coincides with the frontier areas of the time, so for that area we use another circle which coincides with the first. Cincinnati, by the third premise is inside the second circle, which coincides with the first, so it is in the first. The argument so far is valid (See Diagram 5-4). Strictly speaking

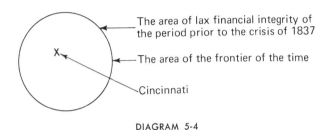

DIAGRAM 5-4

we need to go one step further, for this conclusion is that Cincinnati was in the area of lax financial integrity of the period of the crisis of 1837. The conclusion we seek is that Cincinnati was in an area of lax financial integrity. The move is a simple class reasoning move which I will not diagram.

Step 3. Next the conclusions must be revised in the light of the omitted qualifications in the premises and in the light of knowledge and experience in the field of study. This is Step 3. Certainly the qualifier, 'for the most part', should be reintroduced in the statement of the second conclusion. Turner indicated that he did not want to claim perfect coincidence in area. Other considerations are to be brought to bear, but they can be better illustrated by their application to the third conclusion.

The third conclusion reads as follows:

Cincinnati probably was characterized by lax financial integrity.

First of all if the conclusion is a fact to be explained by Turner's claim, a fact which we accept as true, then the word 'probably' should not be there at all for reasons given earlier.

But suppose that the conclusion is one we derived from Turner's claim (and the other assumptions) in order to test his claim; then presumably the conclusion should be accepted as a conclusion to the argument. If there is as yet no determination of the truth of the implied conclusion, then the word 'probably' should be omitted, because it would indicate qualified endorsement when there should be no endorsement.* But Turner did say

* Please refer back to the discussion of 'probably' earlier in this chapter, if this point is not clear.

"for the most part". He did not strongly commit himself to such a judgment about any particular area. Some sort of qualification would be needed because a determination that Cincinnati had no lax financial integrity should not be allowed by itself to falsify Turner's statement. One might say, "Turner's statement loosely implies that Cincinnati was characterized by lax financial integrity."

After the independent determination of the truth status of the implied conclusion, then what one directly says about it depends upon the determination. One might then assert it without qualification, assert it with qualification, or reject it. But one can still say, "Turner's statement loosely implies that Cincinnati was characterized by lax financial integrity."

Next, suppose that the conclusion is derived in order to get an idea of what life in Cincinnati was like in the early part of the nineteenth century. Here the option is open to the expert to reject the conclusion completely, to accept it with the word 'probably' inserted, or to accept it with no qualifiers. He might reject it completely, if on other grounds he has good reason to believe that it is false. Suppose for example, that we generated such a conclusion about early frontier pilgrim settlements. Having sufficient knowledge about such settlements, an expert would simply reject such a conclusion—with or without 'probably'.

On the other hand, he might accept the conclusion about Cincinnati without the qualifier because the conclusion fits very well with other knowledge that the expert has about Cincinnati at the time. Or he might accept the conclusion with the qualifier included—either because he has some reason to wonder about the conclusion, or because he just does not have sufficient background information to justify an unqualified endorsement of the conclusion. The latter is the situation for most informed laymen. They, more than the experts, should make more liberal use of such words as 'probably', though it is often the other way around.

Summary. In this example one can see the three steps in the practical use of deduction, steps which are interdependent and inseparable in practice. Of particular note are the importance of the context, the provisional elimination of qualifiers during the use of strict deductive techniques, the need for intelligent, informed judgment, the use of another type of logic, and perhaps most important of all, the fact that the hardest part of the practical application of deduction is not the actual use of deductive techniques, but rather the prior and succeeding steps, the steps here numbered 1 and 3.

Supply and demand

Let us move to a different area, economics, and look at the application of one version of the law of supply and demand:

Example 5-12

Premises:

1. Other things being equal, if the demand for a commodity decreases, the price will decrease (assuming that the supply remains the same).
2. The demand for fountain pens is going to decrease.
3. The supply of fountain pens will remain the same.

Conclusion:

The price of fountain pens will probably decrease.

The problems in putting this argument in workable form reside primarily in the first premise. As stated earlier, the general qualifier, "other things being equal", is eliminated* (though later remembered), but the specific qualification dealing with the supply must remain. For convenience, however, it should be put into an 'if' clause. Then the first premise looks like this:

Example 5-13

If the demand for a commodity decreases and the supply remains the same, then the price will decrease.

But more remains to be done. The second and third premises cannot yet be used in conjunction with the first, since it talks about "a commodity" and they talk about fountain pens. This problem was raised before—in the yeast example at the beginning of Chapter 4. The solution at that time was to transform the general sentence into a class sentence. If we use the same method, the first premise, restated in class terms, looks like this:

Example 5-14

Commodities for which the demand decreases as the supply remains the same (are commodities which) will have a decrease in price.

Though awkward, this is a workable version of the first premise. After eliminating 'probably' from the conclusion we can diagram the argument

---

* ∴Alternatively, the general qualification, 'other things being equal', can remain if a premise is added asserting the satisfaction of this qualification. The argument could look like this:

Premises:

1. If the demand for a commodity decreases, the price will decrease, if other things are equal, and if the supply remains the same.
2. The demand for fountain pens is going to decrease.
3. Other things are equal.
4. The supply of fountain pens will remain the same.

Conclusion:

The price of fountain pens will decrease.

In deciding whether to assert Premise 3, one faces many of the same sorts of problems that one faces in deciding whether, or to what extent, to endorse the conclusion.

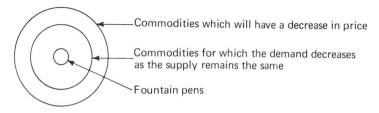

DIAGRAM 5-5

as in Diagram 5-5 (assuming that fountain pens are commodities). The following conclusion can thus be validly derived from the premises:

The price of fountain pens will decrease.

An alternative (and in this case easier) way of reformulating and judging the argument calls for the use of sentence reasoning instead of class reasoning. In order to use sentence reasoning, one must make the explicit instantiating step of putting the conditional premise in terms of fountain pens. We infer from the first premise, as found in Example 5-13, the following instantiation of it:

Example 5-15
If the demand for fountain pens decreases and the supply remains the same, then the price will decrease.

This implication of the first premise together with the two other premises (which are now the antecedent) yields the desired conclusion by means of the valid step, affirmation of the antecedent.

Next comes the most difficult part. The inevitable vagueness of the premises requires a judgment about whether the facts warrant asserting these premises. For example, did the supply remain sufficiently the same to warrant asserting the third premise? The same vagueness problem exists in the conclusion. Will the concluded decrease be sufficient to assert? Furthermore, one must judge whether other things are equal, that is whether other things stay the same. Which other things are involved? All other things? Obviously not—only the relevant ones, and it is only the experienced, informed person who is well qualified to determine which these are. Such factors as lack of price-maintaining agreements by suppliers, advertising campaigns, and national crises* are things that might occur to an ex-

---

* A national crisis, strictly speaking, would negate the qualifier 'under normal conditions' rather than 'other things being equal' in a period of frequent national crises. But since nobody that I know of interprets 'other things being equal' this strictly, I shall not do so; rather I shall conform to standard (and vague) usage and let the phrase be used where 'under normal conditions' would strictly speaking be more appropriate.

perienced, informed person. But even after the expert has made the relevance appraisal, he must still make a judgment about the extent to which the other (relevant) things must stay the same—certainly not absolutely immobile: minor fluctuations can be ignored. Expertise is needed to distinguish minor from significant fluctuations.

As with the argument developing out of one part of Turner's thesis, various courses are open. One is to refuse to affirm the conclusion, perhaps because one believes on other grounds that the conclusion is false or quite dubious, even though one otherwise has good reason to believe that the premises are true. Suppose, for example, that one learns that a number of leading economists have asserted that the price of fountain pens will remain the same.

A second course is to affirm the conclusion but include the word 'probably', because one is not sure enough that something will not go wrong. A third is to affirm the conclusion without the word 'probably', without any qualifications at all. If one has no reason for reservations, and is very well informed, then it is deceptive to include 'probably'.

Note that the use of the future tense in the conclusion ("the price **will** decrease") precludes the possibility of this argument's being part of an explanation. If the past tense had been used and the argument were put forward to explain a fact, then the 'probably' option would not have been open. The first option, that of refusing to affirm the conclusion, would still have been open in the sense that although one accepted the statement given in the conclusion as true, one did not believe that it was explained by the material offered—perhaps because one or more of the premises was believed false. The third option, affirming the conclusion without any qualifiers, is the standard one in the case of explanation.

Neoclassical English writing

Turning to the field of English, consider this argument:

Example 5-16
Premises:
1. English literature of the first fifty years of the eighteenth century was neo-classical.
2. Alexander Pope's *Essay on Man* is English literature written in the first fifty years of the eighteenth century.
Conclusion:
Alexander Pope's *Essay on Man* was probably neoclassical.

Since in this case no explicit changes are required to put the premises into workable form (though the implicit qualifier in the generalization must be ignored when doing the validity test), we can proceed directly to the

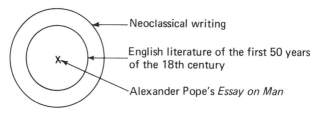

Neoclassical writing

English literature of the first 50 years of the 18th century

Alexander Pope's *Essay on Man*

DIAGRAM 5-6

validity test. The argument is valid as can be seen in Diagram 5-6. Next we turn to the conclusion. Should the word 'probably'* be there even though there is no explicit qualifier in any of the premises?

Think of some possible contexts in which this argument might appear. Realize that even though there are no explicit qualifiers in the generalization, an exception or two will not prove it wrong. Daniel Defoe's *Robinson Crusoe*, for example, which was written in the given period, does not prove the generalization wrong. But a large number of exceptions would prove the generalization wrong. So if this argument is one of a large number which are set up to test the generalization, then we have one conceivable context in which it could be offered. In this context the word 'probably' would not be used, since it indicates endorsement, albeit weak endorsement, by the concluder.

A second context is one in which an English teacher is teaching his students the meaning of the word 'neoclassical' by means of examples. He gives his students the generalization and asks them to go through their memories to find items written by Englishmen in the first half of the eighteenth century. When a student comes up with an example, then the conclusion is drawn, and the student gets a better idea of what the word 'neoclassical' means, in virtue of his having read the item. Here the word 'probably' might be used, or even better, the phrase, 'by this principle'.

A third possible context is that in which an English teacher is trying to teach his students the categorization scheme of the history of literature. And he asks them to apply it to examples that he supplies. He supplies the example. They draw the conclusion and should include 'probably'.

So far as I can see, the argument would not be used in an explanation of why this work of Pope's was neoclassical, though it might be used to explain why someone at a low level of sophistication in the field judges the work to be neoclassical. If this argument is all the reason he has, then he should use 'probably'.

There are other sorts of contexts possible, but we will not go any further.

* Or some similar term, such as 'likely'. In this discussion 'probably' will be used to represent this family of terms.

The main idea is that with this sort of generalization in this field, one should expect exceptions, even though at a given level of sophistication the generalization is to be considered true. Qualifications and endorsements are distributed accordingly, context respected of course.

A body immersed in a fluid

A rather well-known principle of elementary physics, Archimedes' Principle has been stated as follows:

> When a body is totally or partially immersed in a fluid, it experiences an upthrust equal to the weight of fluid displaced.*

A cubic foot of wood held under water will suffice as an illustration of this principle. A cubic foot of wood will displace (occupy the same space as) a cubic foot of water. The weight of a cubic foot of water is given as 62.4 pounds. Hence we can expect, according to the principle, that the wood will experience an upthrust of 62.4 pounds. Suppose that the block of wood itself weighs 50 pounds. Then the force we would have to use to hold down the block of wood would be another 12.4 pounds.

Although this may sound quite simple and straightforward and is quite satisfactory at one level of sophistication, problems can arise, problems that can be seen without an advanced knowledge of physics. Consider this argument which formalizes the first part of reasoning used in the above explanation:

Example 5-17
Premises:
1. When a body is totally or partially immersed in a fluid, it experiences an upthrust equal to the weight of fluid displaced.
2. This cube of wood (measuring one foot on an edge) is totally immersed in this lake water.
3. When a body is totally immersed in a fluid, it displaces an amount of fluid equal to the volume of the body.
4. The weight of one cubic foot of this lake water is 62.4 pounds.
Conclusion:
The block of wood experiences an upthrust of 62.4 pounds.

Ignoring the metaphorical use of 'experience', let us concentrate our attention on the basic moves and problems in this argument. In order to avoid the further complications involved in arriving at the figure of 12.4 pounds downward force, let us limit our concern to the determination of the "upthrust".

* W. Ashhurst, *Physics* (London: John Murray, 1954), p. 35.

Step 1. Since the first premise speaks of "a body" while the second mentions a "cube of wood", the two cannot yet produce a conclusion. We could convert the first premise into a class statement that includes the class of immersed bodies in the class of bodies experiencing the state, upthrust. Alternatively we could instantiate the first premise in terms of this cube of wood and water:

> When this cube of wood is totally or partially immersed in this lake water, it experiences an upthrust equal to the weight of the lake water displaced.

Similarly the third premise can be instantiated:

> When this cube of wood is totally immersed in this lake water, it displaces an amount of water equal to the volume of the block of wood.

In this example I shall use sentence reasoning, making use of these two instantiated premises. There are no explicit general qualifiers in the premises, so Step 1 is complete.

Step 2. The reasoning is straightforward and simple. There is some simple mathematics, which I will simply note without detail. That is the computation of the volume of the cube of wood ($1' \times 1' \times 1' = 1$ cubic foot). This computation enables us to substitute 'one cubic foot' for 'the volume of the block of wood' in the instantiated third premise, since equals may be substituted for equals. The argument now looks like this:

Example 5-18

Premises:
1. When this cube of wood is totally or partially immersed in this lake water, it experiences an upthrust equal to the weight of the lake water displaced.
2. This cube of wood (measuring one foot on an edge) is totally immersed in this lake water.
3. When this cube of wood is totally immersed in this lake water, it displaces an amount of water equal to one cubic foot.
4. The weight of one cubic foot of this lake water is 62.4 pounds.

Conclusion:

This cube of wood experiences an upthrust of 62.4 pounds.

Combining Premise 1 and the affirmation of its antecedent, Premise 2, we get the following:

> 5. This cube of wood experiences an upthrust equal to the weight of the lake water displaced.

Combining Premise 3 and the affirmation of its antecedent, again Premise 2, we get the following:

6. This cube of wood displaces an amount of water equal to 1 cubic foot.

Making use of Premise 4 and substituting equals for equals, Statement 6 becomes:

7. This cube of wood displaces 62.4 pounds of this lake water.

Again substituting equals for equals and using Statement 7, Statement 5 is transformed into the desired conclusion.

The reasoning just described is simple enough for most people to do in their heads. The reason for going through it in detail was to show the operation of various deductive processes. As you know from working on the exercises of Chapters 3 and 4, complications in the reasoning can arise which make doing it in one's head difficult. Note that in addition to sentence reasoning, some mathematical manipulation of numbers was involved, and the equals substitution rule (a deductive rule which is used in many more areas than mathematics) was invoked. Furthermore even to make use of sentence reasoning, adjustments to the two general premises were necessary. They were instantiated.

Step 3. This step brings out the main lessons of the Archimedes example: (1) a degree of imprecision exists in specific predictions in physics and the other precise sciences; (2) unspecified factors can arise (just as in economics) which make the result so wrong that it can no longer be called an approximation; and (3) in areas of familiarity to the engineer, the state of knowledge and precision has advanced to the point that words like 'probably' are often not needed. Let us consider these lessons one at a time.

1. For most ordinary purposes the precision of the conclusion is sufficient, but a number of factors could be taken into account. First, the figure, '62.4', is an approximation. Second the weight of one cubic foot of water varies with the temperature, a factor not mentioned. Also the temperature of the water touching the cube could easily vary from one point to another, thus adding further to the imprecision. In addition, the weight of water depends slightly upon its pressure, which increases with depth. Since the pressure of the water is not constant from top to bottom of the cube of wood, it follows that the weight of the water displaced varies accordingly from top to bottom of the cube. Generally these factors are assumed to be negligible and are ignored. But note that expertise is needed to judge properly that something is negligible.

2. As we approach vastly different situations, then there is always the chance that unspecified factors can arise which throw off the entire estimate. Suppose that there is a continual up current in the lake. The upthrust then increases. This problem is usually handled by using the term 'buoyant force' (a term which covers only the force owing to the actual displacement of the fluid) instead of 'upthrust'. This terminological substitution is a move requiring expertise, for 'buoyant force' is a more theoretical term than 'upthrust'. More serious is the problem encountered when a very small body, say one that is composed of five molecules, is in the lake. Archimedes' Principle was not framed for this kind of case. Even farther removed is the case of one electron shot into the lake. The idea of buoyant force is simply inapplicable, as is the idea of volume, even though the shooting of the electron into the lake might have resulted in the displacement of some amount of water (I am assuming one can give some meaning to 'displacement' here). Thus by rigidly following Archimedes' Principle, one might generate by deduction a prediction which is absurd, even though Archimedes' Principle is true. Hence expertise is called for in deciding whether to endorse a validly deduced conclusion from true premises. Incidentally this case also shows the existence of implicit qualifiers in such principles, at least as they are understood by experts.

3. In spite of the existence of imprecision and the possibility of situational factors which nullify any prediction based on the standard methods of application of such a principle, words like 'probably' are not generally used in such conclusions. This is because within the standard-type situation the result is quite regularly predictable. In modern physics where there is a heavy use of the concept, *probability*, words like 'probably' appear more often. Often in both modern and classical physics some word like 'approximately' is introduced to give warning of the fact that various possibilities for imprecision exist.

The result then in Step 3 varies with the principle and the situation. For cases like the application of Archimedes' Principle to ordinary situations the derived conclusion can often appear without such qualifiers as 'probably' much more often than conclusions in the social sciences and some of the other physical sciences.

Chapter Summary

In this chapter on the practical application of deductive logic the major problems treated are those of putting the premises into a form for dealing with them with deductive techniques, and of deciding whether and how strongly to endorse the conclusion to a piece of practical reasoning.

In putting the premises in workable form one drops such general qualifiers as 'generally', 'other things being equal', 'under normal conditions', etc., but does not omit specific qualifiers like 'if the supply remains the same'. And, of course, one rewords, reorganizes, revises (sometimes this requires drawing out implicit parts) the premises until they fit some logical form with which one can work.

In deciding whether, in what way, and how strongly to endorse the conclusion, one must look at the purpose behind the reasoning (for example: Is it part of an explanation? Is it the basis for a prediction? etc.), and one must look at the field of knowledge for such things as limits beyond which one must be especially careful in applying the generalization, facts which contradict the conclusion or cast suspicion on it, and the sort of context in which the generalization can be fairly safely applied. One also must decide whether the facts are such as to warrant the assertion of the premises.

A related problem is that of finding the appropriate deductive techniques, since the techniques of sentence and class reasoning do not in all cases suffice. Often one can work by analogy to established deductive techniques (which include those of mathematics) and sometimes one must base one's decision simply on the basic rule of deductive argumentation: the denial of the conclusion of a valid deductive argument contradicts the assertion of the premises.

The result of this process can be many things, depending on the purpose behind the reasoning, but very often it is the assertion of, the qualified assertion of, or the deliberate nonassertion of the conclusion. Generally, the strictly logical problem is simpler than the practical application problem.

This chapter does not attempt a thorough comprehensive treatment of the practical application of logic. Instead through the use of a simple model and selected examples it attempts to suggest ways of dealing with the problems faced herein as well as others that appear in other cases. Hopefully, the suggestions will stimulate your ingenuity.

COMPREHENSION SELF-TEST

True or False? If the statement is false, change a crucial term (or terms) to make it true.

5–1. The model put forward here calls for the temporary idealization of an argument in order to make a judgment about its validity.

5–2. In putting an argument into form, one generally eliminates general qualifications from the premises but does not eliminate specific qualifications.

5–3. Rarely does one find a practical deductive argument that requires more than sentence and class reasoning techniques.

5–4. If a deductive argument is used to show how the conclusion of the argument can be explained, then the conclusion should not have the word 'probably' in it.

5–5. Since the practical application of deductive processes is relatively mechanical, anyone with a good knowledge of logic should be able to make the application.

Argument Appraisal out of Context. Take each of the following arguments, put it into form suitable for use of deductive techniques, and judge its validity.

5–6. Premises:
1. Whenever the supply of a commodity increases (assuming that demand remains constant), the price will decrease, other things being equal.

2. It is clear that the price of eggs is going to decrease.
Conclusion:
It follows, therefore, that the supply of eggs is going to increase.

5–7. Frederick Jackson Turner has stated, "The most important effect of the frontier has been in the promotion of democracy here and in Europe." By this he means in part, and says, "The frontier is productive of individualism." Since Turner apparently did not want to limit his analysis to the United States, presumably he would expect to find considerable individualism in the outback of Australia of the present day, for there we find what he would undoubtedly call a frontier.

5–8. A wind shift from south to northwest is generally accompanied by clearing and colder. Since the weather bureau has predicted rain for the next twenty-four hours, quite probably the wind will not shift from south to northwest within twenty-four hours.

5–9. Since English writing of the first fifty years of the eighteenth century was neo-classical, and since Bronte's *Wuthering Heights* is romantic rather than neoclassical, it quite probably was not written in the first fifty years of the eighteenth century.

5–10. The physics book says that a body immersed in a fluid is buoyed up by a force equal to the weight of the fluid displaced. There is a rectangular solid concrete block underwater here which measures $2' \times 2' \times 1'$. Hence there must be a buoyant force of exactly 249.6 pounds on the block.

Argument Appraisal in Context.

5–11. Take one of the above five arguments and imagine and describe a context in which it could appear. Decide whether and how strongly to endorse the conclusion and tell why you judge as you do.

5–12. Find an argument in a book in some subject matter in which you have at least a fair degree of knowledge. Reproduce the argument and write a short essay appraising it. Be sure to include your reasons.

Suggested Further Reading in Logic

The following presentations of deductive logic are arranged roughly in order of increasing difficulty:

Black, Max. *Critical Thinking*, 2nd ed. Englewood Cliffs, N. J.: Prentice-Hall, Inc., 1952. 459 pages.
An elementary, readable, and interesting treatment of deductive logic, scientific method, and semantics. Exercises are provided.

Salmon, Wesley. *Logic*. Englewood Cliffs, N. J.: Prentice-Hall, Inc., 1963. 114 pages.
An elementary book, dealing with deductive logic, scientific method, and semantics. No exercises are provided. The approach to deductive logic differs from that here in that a system of rules is provided for class reasoning. Circles are not used.

Beardsley, Monroe. *Thinking Straight*, 3rd ed. Englewood Cliffs, N. J.: Prentice-Hall, Inc., 1966. 292 pages.

The content is similar to the Black and Salmon books listed above, and is again at an elementary level. Exercises are provided. For class reasoning Venn diagrams are used.

Fisk, Milton. *A Modern Formal Logic*. Englewood Cliffs, N. J.: Prentice-Hall Inc., 1964. 116 pages.

A somewhat more advanced treatment of logic than in the above but still an introductory text. It deals only with deductive logic, and that from the same point of view as that of this book. Exercises are provided.

Copi, Irving. *Introduction to Logic*, 2nd ed. New York: The Macmillan Company, 1961. 472 pages.

An elementary presentation of contemporary symbolic logic. Exercises are provided.

Cohen, Morris, and Ernest Nagel. *An Introduction to Logic and the Scientific Method*. New York: Harcourt, Brace and Company, 1934. 467 pages.

A classic but introductory study of many topics associated with proof. Exercises are provided.

Quine, Willard Van Orman. *Methods of Logic*, rev. ed. New York: Henry Holt and Company, Inc., 1960. 272 pages.

An elegant development of contemporary symbolic logic. Exercises are provided.

❖The following chronologically ordered items are relevant to the ordinary language vs. material (and strict) implication, etc., interpretations of the logical operators:

Whitehead, Alfred North, and Bertrand Russell. *Principia Mathematica*. Cambridge (England): Cambridge University Press, 1910–13.

Lewis, C. I. "Implication and the Algebra of Logic," *Mind*, October, 1912, pp. 522–31.

Lewis, C. I., and C. H. Langford. *Symbolic Logic*. New York: Dover Publications, Inc., 1959 (first published 1932).

Strawson, P. F. *Introduction to Logical Theory*. London: Methuen & Co., Ltd., 1952.

Wright, Georg Henrik von. *Logical Studies*. London (England): Routledge & Kegan Paul, Ltd., 1957.

Smiley, T. J. "Entailment and Deducibility," *Proceedings of the Aristotelian Society*, Vol. 59 (1959), pp. 233–54.

Russell, L. J. "Formal Logic and Ordinary Language," *Analysis*, Vol. 21, No. 2 (December, 1960), pp. 25–34.

Faris, J. A. *Truth-Functional Logic*. New York: The Free Press of Glencoe, 1962 (esp. pp. 107–19).

Anderson, Alan Ross, and Nuel D. Belnap, Jr. "The Pure Calculus of Entailment," *Journal of Symbolic Logic*, Vol. 27 (1962), pp. 19–52.

Bennett, Jonathan. "Entailment," *The Philosophical Review*, Vol. 78, No. 2 (April, 1969), pp. 197-236.

Answers

Assuming that you check the answers only after doing the exercises, the following set of answers can be helpful. Several qualifications and limitations to the use of these answers are in order:

1. Answers to the true-false questions are occasionally debatable. (Differences in the interpretation of some questions sometimes call for answers different from those given.) Make sure you understand whether your answer differs from the one I have suggested as a result of interpretation of the question, or for some other reason.
2. Although you are asked in the exercises to convert false statements into true ones by rewriting, I have not done so here because of the numerous ways of going about it. You can generally judge for yourself whether you have made the appropriate changes.
3. The particular method you use in solving logic problems might well differ from the one offered. Do not automatically abandon yours just because it is different from the method suggested. Yours may well be correct—there are frequently various routes to the solution of logic problems.
4. Since there is often room for differing interpretations of the sentences in the logic exercises, the fact that your judgment about validity differs from that given does not necessarily imply that yours is wrong. However, think very carefully about it before accepting a validity judgment that differs from the one suggested here.

Chapter 2 : "Basic Ideas"

2–1. T   2–2. F   2–3. F

2–4. Valid argument, true premises, and false conclusion.

Chapter 3: "Sentence Reasoning"

3-1. If Mike is a dog, then Mike is an animal.

3-2. Mike is an animal, if Mike is a dog.

3-3. If Mary knows the rules of punctuation, then she did well on the test today.

3-4. If John is nearsighted, his eyes are defective.

3-5. John's eyes are defective, if he is nearsighted.

3-6. If in that sentence the word 'going' is a gerund, then it functions like a noun.

3-7. Mike, if he is a dog, is an animal.

3-8. The soil in your field is sweet, if Jones added the truckload of calcium carbonate to it.

3-9. If the President is not going to veto this bill, the Senate will not stand by him in his efforts to get his tax legislation passed.

3-10. Angles *A* and *B*, if they are alternate interior angles of parallel lines, are equal.

3-11. Joan's room has light-colored walls, if it is well lighted.

3-12. If the music room does not have light-colored walls, then it is not well lighted.

3-13. The livingroom, if Mrs. Smith likes it, is well lighted.

3-14. Denying the consequent. Valid.

3-15. Affirming the consequent. Invalid.

3-16. Affirming the antecedent. Valid.

3-17. Denying the consequent. Valid.

3-18. Affirming the consequent. Invalid.

3-19. Affirming the antecedent. Valid.

3-20. Denying the antecedent. Invalid.

3-21. Joan's room has light-colored walls. Affirming the antecedent (AA).

3-22. Nothing follows necessarily. DA.

3-23. It has light-colored walls. AA.

3-24. The sewing room does not have light-colored walls. DC.

3-25. The kitchen is not well lighted. AA.

3-26. My new office does not have dark-colored walls. DC.

3–27. The music room has light-colored walls. DC.

3–28. The livingroom does not have dark-colored walls. AA; then DC. (Note: An intermediate conclusion [The livingroom is well lighted.] is reached by AA. This conclusion is used as a premise to reach the final conclusion by DC.)

3–29. F   **3–30.** T   **3–31.** T   **3–32.** F

3–33. Converse: If Mike is an animal, then Mike is a dog.
Contrapositive: If Mike is not an animal, then Mike is not a dog.

3–34. Same as 3–33.

3–35. Converse: If Mary did well on the test today, then she knows the rules of punctuation.
Contrapositive: If Mary did not do well on the test today, then she does not know the rules of punctuation.

3–36. Converse: If John's eyes are defective, then he is nearsighted.
Contrapositive: If John's eyes are not defective, then he is not nearsighted.

3–37. Same as 3–36.

3–38. Converse: If it functions like a noun, then the word 'going' in that sentence is a gerund.
Contrapositive: If it does not function like a noun, then the word 'going' in that sentence is not a gerund.

3–39. Same as 3–33.

3–40. Converse: If the soil in your field is sweet, then Jones added the truckload of calcium carbonate to it.
Contrapositive: If the soil in your field is not sweet, then Jones did not add the truckload of calcium carbonate to it.

3–41. Converse: If the Senate will not stand by him in his efforts to get his tax legislation passed, then the President is not going to veto the bill.
Contrapositive: If the Senate will stand by him in his efforts to get his tax legislation passed, then the President is going to veto the bill.

3–42. Converse: If angles A and B are equal, then they are alternate interior angles of parallel lines.
Contrapositive: If angles A and B are not equal, then they are not alternate interior angles of parallel lines.

3–43. Converse: If Joan's room has light-colored walls, then it is well lighted.
Contrapositive: If Joan's room does not have light-colored walls, then it is not well lighted.

3–44. Converse: If the music room is not well lighted, then it does not have light-colored walls.
Contrapositive: If the music room is well lighted, then it has light-colored walls.

3–45. Converse: If the livingroom is well lighted, then Mrs. Smith likes it.
Contrapositive: If the livingroom is not well lighted, then Mrs. Smith does not like it.

3–46. Valid. Contraposition.

3-47. Invalid. Conversion.

3-48. Valid. Double negation and AA. (Note: The principle of double negation is used to convert the second premise to an affirmed antecedent of the first premise.)

3-49. Invalid. AC.

3-50. Valid. DC.

3-51. Valid. AA.

3-52. Invalid. DA.

3-53. Valid. Contraposition.

3-54. Invalid. Conversion.

3-55. Valid. Contraposition.

3-56. Invalid. Conversion (of the contrapositive).

3-57. T   **3-58.** F   **3-59.** T   **3-60.** T   **3-61.** F

3-62. Worked as an example.

3-63. Let 'p' = 'Jones is President'
Let 'q' = 'Jones must be at least thirty-five years of age'
Premises:
$$p \longrightarrow q$$
$$p$$
Conclusion:
$$q$$
Valid. AA.

3-64. Let 'p' = 'This figure is an equilateral triangle'
Let 'q' = 'It has all sides equal'
Premises:
$$p \longrightarrow q$$
$$\text{not } q$$
Conclusion:
$$\text{not } p$$
Valid. DC.

3-65. Let 'p' = 'These two plants are not closely related'
Let 'q' = 'They can not be crossed'
Premises:
$$p \longrightarrow q$$
$$\text{not } p$$
Conclusion:
$$\text{not } q$$
Invalid. DA.

3-66. Let 'p' = 'There is no light reaching it'
Let 'q' = 'Photosynthesis can not occur in this plant'
Premises:
$$p \longrightarrow q$$
$$p$$

Conclusion:

    q

Valid. AA.

3-67. Let 'p' = 'Great Birnam wood to high Dunsinane hill shall come against him'

Let 'q' = 'Macbeth shall be vanquished'

Premises:

    not $p \longrightarrow$ not q

    not p

Conclusion:

    not q

Valid. AA.

3-68. Let 'p' = 'The beacon is lit'

Let 'q' = 'You may not fly'

Premises:

    $p \longrightarrow q$

    not p

Conclusion:

    not q

Invalid. DA.

3-69. Let 'p' = 'Senator Franklin will oppose the tax legislation'

Let 'q' = 'Senator Inkling will vote in favor of it'

Let 'r' = 'My wife will be busy trying to . . . to help defeat him at the polls'

Let 's' = 'Dinners will not be very good around here for a while'

Part 1:

    Premises:

        p

        $p \longrightarrow q$

    Conclusion:

        q

    Valid. AA.

Part 2:

    Premises:

        q (from Part 1)

        $q \longrightarrow r$

    Conclusion:

        r

    Valid. AA.

Part 3:

    Premises:

        r (from Part 2)

        $r \longrightarrow s$

    Conclusion:

        s

    Valid. AA.

(I am willing to assume that 's' is essentially the same as the conclusion announced in the last sentence. Are you? If this is acceptable, the total argument is valid.)

3–70. Let 'p' = 'The Board of Education suspends young Brown from school'
   Let 'q' = 'It will be punishing him for refusing to salute the flag on religious grounds'
   Let 'r' = 'It will be acting unconstitutionally'
   Part 1:
       Premises:
           not r
           $q \longrightarrow r$
       Conclusion:
           not q
       Valid DC.
   Part 2:
       Premises:
           not q (from Part 1)
           $p \longrightarrow q$
       Conclusion:
           not p
       Valid. DC.
   Hence the total argument is valid.

3–71. Antecedent.   **3–72.** $p \longrightarrow q$.   **3–73.** q.

3–74. Valid.   **3–75.** Consequent.   **3–76.** Not q.

3–77. Not p.   **3–78.** Affirming.   **3–79.** Consequent.

3–80. p.*   **3–81.** Invalid.   **3–82.** Denying.**

3–83. Antecedent.   **3–84.** Not p.   **3–85.** Nothing.

3–86. Invalid.

3–87. T   **3–88.** T   **3–89.** F   **3–90.** T   **3–91.** F

3–92. T   **3–93.** F   **3–94.** T   **3–95.** T

3–96. Let 'p' = 'Your report is satisfactory'
   Let 'q' = 'every word is spelled correctly'
   Premises:
       $p \longrightarrow q$
       not p
   Conclusion:
       not q
   Invalid. DA.

3–97. Let 'p' = 'triangles A and B are congruent'
   Let 'q' = 'they have two angles and the included side equal'
   Premises:
       $p \longleftrightarrow q$
       not p

---

* Note that as the question calls for argument forms, one must in answering give a conclusion, so that the argument can be properly termed invalid.
** The question asks for the **four** basic forms of conditional argument. As you have already given three of these forms, the fourth is called for.

Conclusion:

  not q

Valid. Biconditional yields '$q \longrightarrow p$'. DC.

3–98. Let 'p' = 'the lighting in the livingroom is not indirect'
Let 'q' = 'it is not satisfactory'
Let 'r' = 'Mrs. Smith will not like it'
Premises:

  $p \longrightarrow q$
  $q \longrightarrow r$

Conclusion:

  $p \longrightarrow r$

Valid. Conditional chain.

3–99. Let 'p' = 'Shakespeare had intended Polonius to be a comic figure'

Let 'q' = 'he would not have made Polonius the father of two tragic characters'

Premises:

  $p \longrightarrow q$
  not q

Conclusion:

  not p

Valid. DC.

3–100. Let 'p' = 'Governor Jones signed the letter'
Let 'q' = 'serious damage to his chances for the Vice-Presidency was permitted by his advisers'
Let 'r' = 'they did not really want him to be candidate for the Vice-Presidency'
Premises:

  $p \longrightarrow q$
  $q \longrightarrow r$

Conclusion:

  $p \longrightarrow r$

Valid. Conditional chain.

3–101. Let 'p' = 'the ceiling is not one thousand feet or above'
Let 'q' = 'you may not fly'
Let 'r' = 'the sequence report reads less than "10" '
Premises:

  $p \longrightarrow q$
  $r \longleftrightarrow p$
  not r

Intermediate conclusion:

  not p

Valid. Biconditional yields '$p \longrightarrow r$'. DC.

Final conclusion:
    not q
Invalid. DA.

Note that 3–101 was broken up into parts in a different way from that used in 3–69 and 3–70. This variation illustrates the fact that various equally satisfactory ways can be used to analyze an argument, especially a complex one.

3–102. Let 'p' = 'he spells words as they sound to him'
Let 'q' = 'he spells "trough" as "troff"'
Let 'r' = 'he spells "didn't" as "ding"'
Premises:
    $q \longrightarrow p$
    $p \longrightarrow r$
    not q
    r
Conclusion:
    p
Invalid. DA or AC.

3–103. Let 'p' = 'plants X and Y can be crossed'
Let 'q' = 'they are closely related'
Let 'r' = 'their immediate parents have produced hybrids in the past'
Premises:
    $p \longrightarrow q$
    $r \longrightarrow$ not p
    not r
Conclusion:
    q
Invalid. DA. (Note: The attempt to arrive at an intermediate conclusion, p, and then to try to derive the secondary conclusion, q, would not succeed, since the denial of r is the denial of an antecedent.)

3–104. p is sufficient for q. (or q is necessary for p) (3–96)

3–105. p is necessary and sufficient for q. (or q is necessary and sufficient for p) (3–97)

3–106. p is sufficient for q. (or q is necessary for p) (3–98)
q is sufficient for r. (or r is necessary for q)
p is sufficient for r. (or r is necessary for p)

3–107. p is sufficient for q. (or q is necessary for p) (3–99)

3–108. p is sufficient for q. (or q is necessary for p) (3–100)
q is sufficient for r. (or r is necessary for q)
p is sufficient for r. (or r is necessary for p)

3–109. p is sufficient for q. (or q is necessary for p) (3–101)
r is necessary and sufficient for p. (or p is necessary and sufficient for r)

3–110. q is sufficient for p. (or p is necessary for q) (3–102)
p is sufficient for r. (or r is necessary for p)

3–111. p is sufficient for q. (or q is necessary for p) (3–103)
r is sufficient for the falsity of p. (or the falsity of p is necessary for r)

3-112. T   **3-113.** T   **3-114.** T   **3-115.** F   **3-116.** T   **3-117.** T

3-118. Let '*p*' = 'this piece of cloth is warm'
Let '*q*' = 'it is only 50 per cent wool'
p and *q*

3-119. Same symbolization as 3-118.
p and *q*

3-120. Let '*p*' = 'Thomas Jefferson was a scholar'
Let '*q*' = 'he was a gentleman'
Let '*r*' = 'he was an astute politician'
p and *q* and *r*

3-121. Let '*p*' = 'there will be rain within the week'
Let '*q*' = 'the crops will be ruined'
p or *q*

3-122. Let '*p*' = 'the two colors that you select will match'
Let '*q*' = 'the room will be ugly'
p or *q*

3-123. Let '*p*' = 'that figure is a square'
Let '*q*' = 'it does not have four sides'
p or *q* (Even though the content justifies strong alternation. In some
contexts '*p* or *q*' would be an acceptable interpretation.)

3-124. Let '*p*' = 'there is now a rainbow'
Let '*q*' = 'there is now a completely overcast sky'
Not both *p* and *q*

3-125. Let '*p*' = 'Abraham Lincoln thought that his Gettysburg Address was reverently received'
Let '*q*' = 'he thought it was a failure'
p or *q*

3-126. Let '*p*' = '*Alice in Wonderland* is a book for children'
Let '*q*' = 'it is also a book for adults'
p and *q*

3-127. Let '*p*' = 'Hamlet was in doubt of the guilt of his uncle'
Let '*q*' = 'Hamlet was convinced that he had actually spoken to his father's
ghost'
not both *p* and *q*

3-128. If there is not rain within the week, the crops will be ruined.

3-129. If the two colors that you select will not match, then the room will be ugly.

3-130. If that figure is not a square, it does not have four sides.

3-131. If Abraham Lincoln did not think that his Gettysburg Address was reverently
received, then he thought it was a failure.

3-132. Let '*p*' = 'this piece of cloth is warm'
Let '*q*' = 'it is 50 per cent wool'
Let '*r*' = 'the dog is shivering from cold'

Premises:
    p and q
    $r \longrightarrow$ not p
Conclusion:
    not r
Valid. DC.

3–133. Let 'p' = 'the label on this piece of cloth reads "50 per cent" wool'
Let 'q' = 'it is 50 per cent wool'
Let 'r' = 'the piece of cloth is warm'
Premises:
    r and q
    $p \longrightarrow q$
Conclusion:
    p
Invalid. AC.

3–134. Let 'p' = 'he was a scholar'
Let 'q' = 'he was a gentleman'
Let 'r' = 'he was an astute politician'
Let 's' = 'he made the mistake of which you are accusing him'
Premises:
    $s \longrightarrow$ not r
    p and q and r
Conclusion:
    not s
Valid. DC.

3–135. Let 'p' = 'there will be rain within the week'
Let 'q' = 'the crops will be ruined'
Premises:
    p or q
    not p
Conclusion:
    q
Valid. Denial of alternant.

3–136. Let 'p' = 'the two colors that you select will match'
Let 'q' = 'the room will be ugly'
Let 'r' = 'I help you select the colors'
Premises:
    p or q
    $r \longrightarrow p$
    r
Intermediate conclusion:
    p
Valid. Affirming the antecedent
Final conclusion:
    not q
Invalid. Affirmation of an alternant.

3–137. Let 'p' = 'that figure is a square'
Let 'q' = 'it does not have four sides'
Premises:
p or q
not p
Conclusion:
q
Valid. Denial of alternant.

3–138. Let 'p' = 'there is now a rainbow'
Let 'q' = 'there is now a completely overcast sky'
Premises:
not both p and q
q
Conclusion:
not p
Valid. Affirmation of negajunct.

3–139. Let 'p' = 'Abraham Lincoln thought that his Gettysburg Address was reverently received'
Let 'q' = 'he thought it was a failure'
Premises:
p or q
not p
Conclusion:
q
Valid. Denial of alternant.

3–140. Let 'p' = 'Jones likes *Alice in Wonderland*'
Let 'q' = 'it is not a book for children'
Let 'r' = 'it is also a book for adults'
Premises:
$p \longrightarrow q$
not q
r
Conclusion:
p
Invalid. The valid conclusion is 'not p', by denial of consequent. Hence the conclusion given actually contradicts the validly drawn conclusion.

3–141. Let 'p' = 'Hamlet was in doubt about the guilt of his uncle'
Let 'q' = 'Hamlet was convinced that he had actually spoken to his father's ghost'
Premises:
not both p and q
q
Conclusion:
not p
Valid. Affirmation of negajunct.

3–142. F   **3–143.** T   **3–144.** T   **3–145.** T.

3–146. (3–66), (using previous symbolization)

Statements:
1. $p \longrightarrow q$
2. p
3. q

Reasons:
1. Premise
2. Premise
3. 1, 2, AA

3–147. (3–67)

Statements:
1. not $p \longrightarrow$ not q
2. not p
3. not q

Reasons:
1. Premise
2. Premise
3. 1, 2, AA

3–148. (3–68)

Statements:
1. $p \longrightarrow q$
2. not p
3. ?

Reasons:
1. Premise
2. Premise
3. 1, 2, DA

3–149. (3–69)

Statements:
1. p
2. $p \longrightarrow q$
3. $q \longrightarrow r$
4. $r \longrightarrow s$
5. q
6. r
7. s

Reasons:
1. Premise
2. Premise
3. Premise
4. Premise
5. 1, 2, AA
6. 3, 5, AA
7. 4, 6, AA

(Note that this one can also be done just as easily with the conditional chain principle.)

3–150. (3–70)

Statements:
1. not r
2. $q \longrightarrow r$
3. $p \longrightarrow q$
4. not q
5. not p

Reasons:
1. Premise
2. Premise
3. Premise
4. 1, 2, DC
5. 3, 4, DC

3–151. (3–96)

Statements:
1. $p \longrightarrow q$
2. not p
3. ?

Reasons:
1. Premise
2. Premise
3. 1, 2, DA

3–152. (3–97)

Statements:
1. $p \longleftrightarrow q$
2. not p
3. $q \longrightarrow p$
4. not q

Reasons:
1. Premise
2. Premise
3. 1, constituent of biconditional
4. 2, 3, DC

3–153. (3–98)

Statements:
1. $p \rightarrow q$
2. $q \rightarrow r$
3. $p \rightarrow r$

Reasons:
1. Premise
2. Premise
3. 1, 2, conditional chain

3–154. (3–99)

Statements:
1. $p \rightarrow q$
2. not q
3. not p

Reasons:
1. Premise
2. Premise
3. 1, 2, DC

3–155. (3–100)

Statements:
1. $p \rightarrow q$
2. $q \rightarrow r$
3. $p \rightarrow r$

Reasons:
1. Premise
2. Premise
3. 1, 2, conditional chain

3–156. (3–101)

Statements:
1. $p \rightarrow q$
2. $r \leftrightarrow p$
3. not r
4. $p \rightarrow r$

5. not p
6. ?

Reasons:
1. Premise
2. Premise
3. Premise
4. 2, biconditional yields constituent
5. 3, 4, DC
6. 1, 5, DA

3–157. (3–102)

Statements:
1. $q \rightarrow p$
2. $p \rightarrow r$
3. not q
4. r
5. ?

Reasons:
1. Premise
2. Premise
3. Premise
4. Premise
5. 1, 3, DA or 2, 4, AC

3–158. (3–103)

Statements:
1. $p \rightarrow q$
2. $r \rightarrow$ not p
3. not r
4. ?

Reasons:
1. Premise
2. Premise
3. Premise
4. 2, 3, DA

3–159. (3–135)

Statements:
1. p or q
2. not p
3. q

Reasons:
1. Premise
2. Premise
3. 1, 2, denial of alternant

3–160. (3–136)

Statements:
1. p or q
2. $r \rightarrow p$

Reasons:
1. Premise
2. Premise

      3. r 3. Premise
      4. p 4. 2, 3, AA
      5. ?   5. 1, 4, affirmation of alternant

3–161. (3–137)
      Statements: Reasons:
        1. p or q 1. Premise
        2. not p 2. Premise
        3. q 3. 1, 2, denial of alternant

3–162. (3–138)
      Statements: Reasons:
        1. not both p and q 1. Premise
        2. q 2. Premise
        3. not p 3. 1, 2, affirmation of negajunct.

3–163. (3–139)
      Statements: Reasons:
        1. p or q 1. Premise
        2. not p 2. Premise
        3. q 3. 1, 2, denial of alternant

3–164. (3–140)
      Statements: Reasons:
        1. $p \longrightarrow q$ 1. Premise
        2. not q 2. Premise
        3. r 3. Premise
        4. not p 4. 1, 2, DC
This statement at Step 4 contradicts the suggested conclusion, which therefore
is not appropriate.

3–165. (3–141)
      Statements: Reasons:
        1. not both p and q 1. Premise
        2. q 2. Premise
        3. not p 3. 1, 2, affirmation of negajunct

3–166. Statements: Reasons:
        1. $p \longrightarrow q$ 1. Premise
        2. $q \longrightarrow r$ 2. Premise
        3. $r \longrightarrow s$ 3. Premise
        4. $s \longrightarrow t$ 4. Premise
        5. $t \longrightarrow v$ 5. Premise
        6. $p \longrightarrow r$ 6. 1, 2, conditional chain
        7. $p \longrightarrow s$ 7. 3, 6, conditional chain
        8. $p \longrightarrow t$ 8. 4, 7, conditional chain
        9. $p \longrightarrow v$ 9. 5, 8, conditional chain

3–167. F   **3–168.** T   **3–169.** T   **3–170.** F   **3–171.** T.

3–172. and **3–181.**
      Let 'p' $=$ 'Governor Smith is actually planning to throw his hat in the ring'
      Let 'q' $=$ 'the reporters asked him to declare himself'
      Let 'r' $=$ 'he has refused to do so'

Statements: Reasons:
   1. $p \longrightarrow (q \longrightarrow r)$ (3–172)   1. Premise
   2. p 2. Premise
   3. not r 3. Premise
   4. $q \longrightarrow r$ 4. 1, 2, AA
   5. not q 5. 3, 4, DC

3–173. (same symbolization assignment as 3–172)

    $p \longrightarrow$ (not q or r)

3–174. (same assignment as 3–172)

    $(p$ and $q) \longrightarrow r$

3–175. and **3–182.**

Let 'p' = 'Iceland has ordered the fishing vessels of Great Britain to leave the area within ten miles of Iceland's shores'

Let 'q' = 'Iceland is sovereign in that ten-mile zone'

Let 'r' = 'the ships of Britain leave'

Statements: Reasons:
   1. $p \longrightarrow (q \longrightarrow r)$ (3–175)   1. Premise
   2. p 2. Premise
   3. r 3. Premise
   4. $q \longrightarrow r$ 4. 1, 2, AA
   5. ?   5. 3, 4, AC

3–176. (same assignment as 3–175)

    $p \longrightarrow (r \longrightarrow q)$

3–177 and **3–183.**

Let 'p' = 'Jones is given the *California Test of Mental Maturity* under standard conditions'

Let 'q' = 'his IQ is about 100'

Let 'r' = 'his score is about 100'

Let 's' = 'Jones knows calculus'

Statements: Reasons:
    1. $p \longrightarrow (q \longleftrightarrow r)$ (3–177)   1. Premise
    2. not both s and q 2. Premise
    3. s 3. Premise
    4. r 4. Premise
    5. not q 5. 2, 3, affirmation of negajunct
  *6. p 6. Assumption
  *7. $q \longleftrightarrow r$ 7. 1, 6, AA
  *8. $r \longrightarrow q$ 8. 7, constituent of biconditional
  *9. q 9. 4, 8, AA
 *10. q and not q 10. 5, 9
  11. not p 11. 10, indirect proof

Note that a separate step (number 10) was used to assert the contradiction. Example 3–36 in the text did not do so. Either way is all right.

3–178 and **3–184.**

Let 'p' = 'you put this mercury thermometer in the beaker of water'

Let 'q' = 'the thermometer read x'

Let 'r' = 'the temperature was x'

Statements: Reasons:

1. $p \rightarrow (q \leftrightarrow r)$ (3–178)   1. Premise

2. p 2. Premise

3. q 3. Premise

4. $q \leftrightarrow r$ 4. 1, 2, AA

5. r 5. 3, 4, AA

3–179 and **3–185.**

Let 'p' = 'this small piece of dough is put in the warming pan'

Let 'q' = 'this small piece of dough will double in size in twenty minutes'

Let 'r' = 'the dough on the board will not rise sufficiently'

Let 's' = 'the dough is put in the oven'

Statements: Reasons:

1. $p \rightarrow (q$ or $(s \rightarrow r))$ (3–179)   1. Premise

2. p 2. Premise

3. not q 3. Premise

4. s 4. Premise

5. q or $(s \rightarrow r)$ 5. 1, 2, AA

6. $s \rightarrow r$ 6. 3, 5, denial of alternant

7. r 7. 4, 6, AA

3–180 and **3–186.**

Let 'p' = 'lines AB and CD are not parallel to each other'

Let 'q' = 'a third line is drawn in the same plane'

Let 'r' = 'it will cross one and only one of them'

Let 's' = 'it will cross both of them'

Statements: Reasons:

  1. $p \rightarrow (q \rightarrow (r$ or $s))$ (3–180)   1. Premise

  2. q 2. Premise

  3. not r 3. Premise

  4. not s 4. Premise

*5. p 5. Assumption

*6. $q \rightarrow (r$ or $s)$ 6. 1, 5, AA

*7. r or s 7. 2, 6, AA

*8. s 8. 3, 7, denial of alternant

*9. s and not s 9. 4, 8

 10. not p 10. 9, indirect proof

3–187. Let 'p' = 'X was rubbed on Y'

Let 'q' = 'X is harder than Y'

Let 'r' = 'X scratched Y'

Let 's' = 'there are marks on Y'

Statements: Reasons:

1. $p \rightarrow (q \leftrightarrow r)$ 1. Premise

2. $r \rightarrow s$ 2. Premise

3. p	3. Premise
4. s	4. Premise
5. $q \leftrightarrow r$	5. 1, 3, AA
6. ?	6. 2, 4, AC

3–188. Let 'p' = 'this pronoun is the object of a preposition'
Let 'q' = 'it requires the objective form'
Let 'r' = 'it should appear as "him"'
Let 's' = 'It appears as "he"'
Let 't' = 'the sentence is in error'

Statements: Reasons:

1. $p \rightarrow q$	1. Premise
2. $q \rightarrow r$	2. Premise
3. (s and r) $\rightarrow t$	3. Premise
*4. s and p	4. Assumption
*5. q	5. 1, 4, AA
*6. r	6. 2, 5, AA
*7. t	7. 3, 4, 6, AA
8. (s and p) $\rightarrow t$	8. 4, 7, conditional proof

3–189. Let 'p' = 'Communism is going to spread in Lower Slobbovia'
Let 'q' = 'the Prime Minister was defeated in the recent election'
Let 'r' = 'there has been an announcement of his defeat in the local newspaper'
Let 's' = 'the Lower Slobbovians are discontent'

Statements: Reasons:

1. $p \rightarrow q$	1. Premise
2. $q \rightarrow r$	2. Premise
3. not r	3. Premise
4. s	4. Premise
5. not q	5. 2, 3, DC
6. not p	6. 1, 5, DC
*7. $s \rightarrow p$	7. Assumption
*8. p	8. 4, 7, AA
*9. p and not p	9. 6, 8
10. not ($s \rightarrow p$)	10. 9, indirect proof

3–190. Let 'p' = 'the wind is not from the east'
Let 'q' = 'the contour lines are close together'
Let 'r' = 'the hill is steep'
Let 's' = 'there is turbulence on the west side'
Let 't' = 'the wind is from the west'
Let 'u' = 'we will have a good race course close to the west shore'
Let 'v' = 'we must have our race on a triangular course with two buoys on the east shore'

Statements: Reasons:

1. p	1. Premise
2. $q \leftrightarrow r$	2. Premise
3. $t \rightarrow (r \rightarrow s)$	3. Premise

4. not both s and u	4. Premise
5. not $u \longrightarrow v$	5. Premise
6. q	6. Premise
7. r	7. 2, 6, AA
*8. t	8. Assumption
*9. $r \longrightarrow s$	9. 3, 8, AA
*10. s	10. 7, 9, AA
*11. not u	11. 4, 10, affirmation of negajunct
*12. v	12. 5, 11, AA
13. $t \longrightarrow v$	13. 8, 12, conditional proof

Chapter 4: "Class Reasoning"

4–1. F   **4–2.** F   **4–3.** T

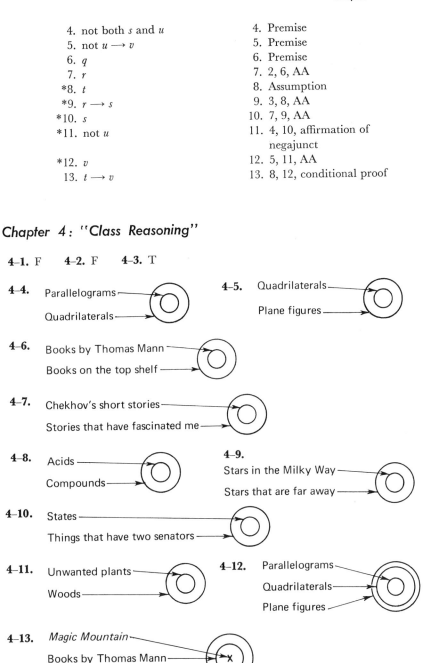

4–4. Parallelograms / Quadrilaterals

4–5. Quadrilaterals / Plane figures

4–6. Books by Thomas Mann / Books on the top shelf

4–7. Chekhov's short stories / Stories that have fascinated me

4–8. Acids / Compounds

4–9. Stars in the Milky Way / Stars that are far away

4–10. States / Things that have two senators

4–11. Unwanted plants / Woods

4–12. Parallelograms / Quadrilaterals / Plane figures

4–13. *Magic Mountain* / Books by Thomas Mann / Books on the top shelf

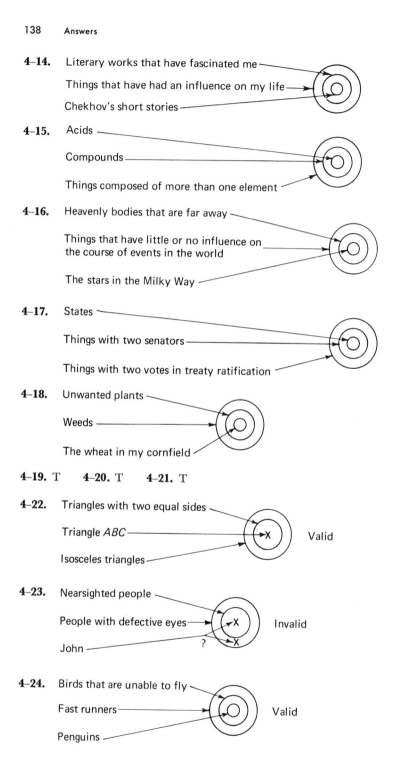

4-14. Literary works that have fascinated me

Things that have had an influence on my life

Chekhov's short stories

4-15. Acids

Compounds

Things composed of more than one element

4-16. Heavenly bodies that are far away

Things that have little or no influence on the course of events in the world

The stars in the Milky Way

4-17. States

Things with two senators

Things with two votes in treaty ratification

4-18. Unwanted plants

Weeds

The wheat in my cornfield

4-19. T   **4-20.** T   **4-21.** T

4-22. Triangles with two equal sides

Triangle *ABC*

Isosceles triangles

Valid

4-23. Nearsighted people

People with defective eyes

John

Invalid

4-24. Birds that are unable to fly

Fast runners

Penguins

Valid

4–25.

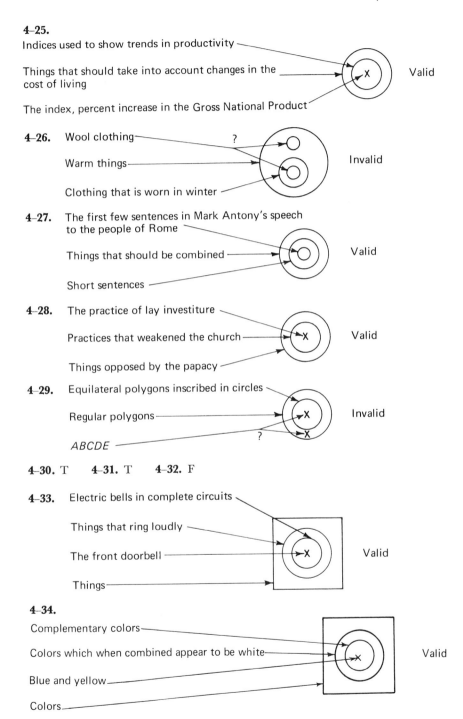

Indices used to show trends in productivity

Things that should take into account changes in the cost of living   X   Valid

The index, percent increase in the Gross National Product

4–26.   Wool clothing   ?

Warm things   Invalid

Clothing that is worn in winter

4–27.   The first few sentences in Mark Antony's speech to the people of Rome

Things that should be combined   Valid

Short sentences

4–28.   The practice of lay investiture

Practices that weakened the church   X   Valid

Things opposed by the papacy

4–29.   Equilateral polygons inscribed in circles

Regular polygons   X   Invalid

ABCDE   ?   X

4–30. T   **4–31.** T   **4–32.** F

4–33.   Electric bells in complete circuits

Things that ring loudly

The front doorbell   X   Valid

Things

4–34.

Complementary colors

Colors which when combined appear to be white   X   Valid

Blue and yellow

Colors

4-35.

Men who are not trusted by the American people

Men who are not elected president

Men

Valid

4-36.   Bells in complete circuits

Things that ring loudly

The bell in my hand

Things

Invalid

4-37.

Men who are elected president by the American people

Men who are trusted by the American people

Blaine

Men

Valid

4-38.

Plants and animals which are not closely related

Things which cannot be crossed to produce hybrids

Plants X and Y

Things

Valid

4-39.

People who know the proper rules of punctuation

People who do well in their written compositions

Mary

People

Valid

4-40.   True believers

Heretics

Condemned people

People

Invalid

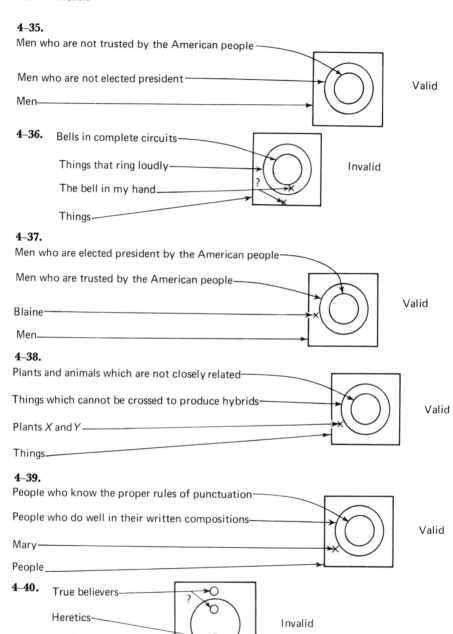

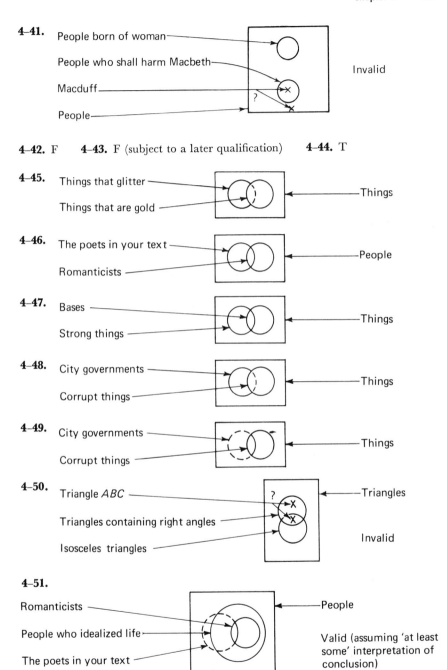

4-41.
People born of woman

People who shall harm Macbeth

Macduff

People

Invalid

4-42. F   **4-43.** F (subject to a later qualification)   **4-44.** T

4-45.
Things that glitter

Things that are gold

Things

4-46.
The poets in your text

Romanticists

People

4-47.
Bases

Strong things

Things

4-48.
City governments

Corrupt things

Things

4-49.
City governments

Corrupt things

Things

4-50.
Triangle *ABC*

Triangles containing right angles

Isosceles triangles

Triangles

Invalid

4-51.
Romanticists

People who idealized life

The poets in your text

People

Valid (assuming 'at least some' interpretation of conclusion)

4-52.

Plants in which photosynthesis occurs

Plants in which photosynthesis does not occur

Things that need water

Things

Invalid

4-53.

Foods

Things containing hydrogen and oxygen

Carbohydrates

Things

Invalid

4-54.

Things that glitter

Gold things

Trinkets in this box

Things

Invalid

4-55.

City goverments

Corrupt institutions

The goverment of New York

Institutions

Invalid

4-56.

The liquid I spilled on my lab table

Bases

Strong substances

Substances

Invalid

4-57.

People who voted for Senator Smart

People who voted against themselves

Fools

John Brown

People

Valid

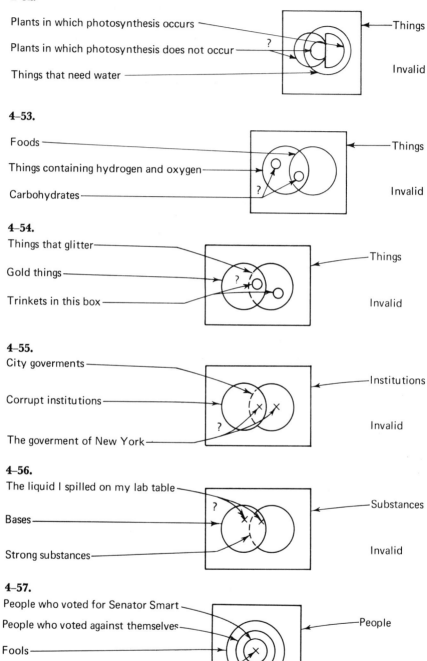

4-58.

Genuine foods

Substances containing hydrogen and
                      oxygen

Carbohydrates

Substances containing carbon

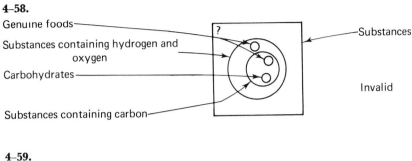

Substances

Invalid

4-59.

People who have done what they have done
as a result of their own inherent greatness

People who have attained historical fame

Characters in the history book

Napoleon Bonaparte

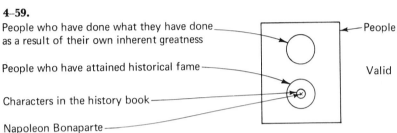

People

Valid

Note: Lewis Carroll's problems can be handled in a number of ways. One good strategy is to try to develop a series of concentric circles—at most two series of such circles.

4-60.

Babies

Illogical people

Despised people

People who cannot handle crocodiles

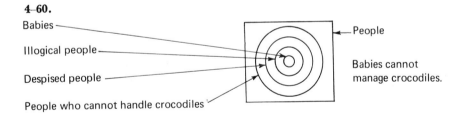

People

Babies cannot
manage crocodiles.

4-61.

Non-well-written books

Unbound books

Books not recommended by me

Unhealthy books

Nonromances

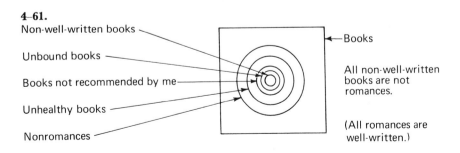

Books

All non-well-written
books are not
romances.

(All romances are
well-written.)

4-62.

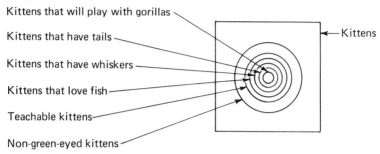

Kittens that will play with gorillas

Kittens that have tails

Kittens that have whiskers

Kittens that love fish

Teachable kittens

Non-green-eyed kittens

Kittens

Kittens that will play with gorillas do not have green eyes.

4-63.

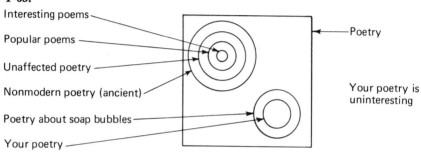

Interesting poems

Popular poems

Unaffected poetry

Nonmodern poetry (ancient)

Poetry about soap bubbles

Your poetry

Poetry

Your poetry is uninteresting

4-64. T   **4-65.** F   **4-66.** T

4-67.

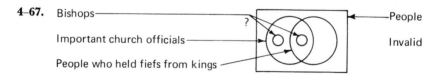

Bishops

Important church officials

People who held fiefs from kings

People

Invalid

4-68.

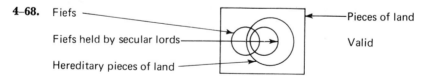

Fiefs

Fiefs held by secular lords

Hereditary pieces of land

Pieces of land

Valid

4-69.

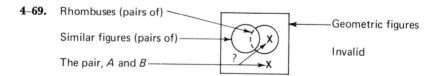

Rhombuses (pairs of)

Similar figures (pairs of)

The pair, A and B

Geometric figures

Invalid

4-70.

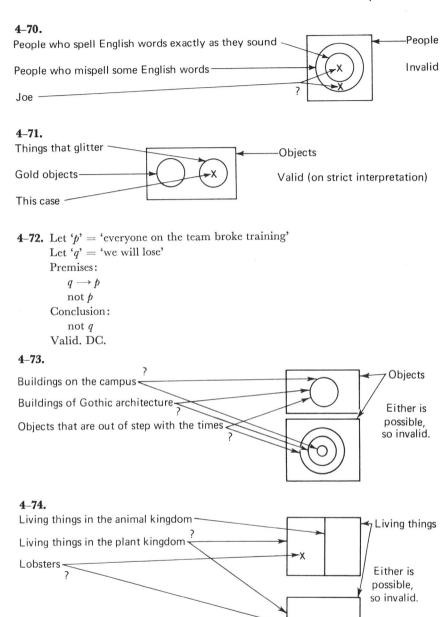

People who spell English words exactly as they sound

People who mispell some English words

Joe

—People

Invalid

4-71.

Things that glitter

Gold objects

This case

—Objects

Valid (on strict interpretation)

4-72. Let 'p' = 'everyone on the team broke training'
Let 'q' = 'we will lose'
Premises:
$q \longrightarrow p$
not p
Conclusion:
not q
Valid. DC.

4-73.

Buildings on the campus

Buildings of Gothic architecture

Objects that are out of step with the times

Objects

Either is possible, so invalid.

4-74.

Living things in the animal kingdom

Living things in the plant kingdom

Lobsters

Living things

Either is possible, so invalid.

4–75. Let '*p*' = 'the present municipal airport should continue to be used for purposes of general aviation'

Let '*q*' = 'it should be used to provide a site for a summer festival every year'

Let '*r*' = 'the other airport is to be closed down'

Premises:

   p (or) *q*

   p ⟶ *r*

   not *r*

Subconclusion (from the second and third premises):

   not *p*

Valid. DC.

Conclusion:

   q

Valid. Denial of alternant.

4–76. Let '*p*' = 'Brown has a position on the Rules Committee'

Let '*q*' = 'all the men on this list have declined to serve'

Let '*r*' = 'Jones is on this list'

Let '*s*' = 'Jones has declined to serve'

Let '*t*' = 'Jones was appointed to the Appropriations Committee'

Premises:

   p ⟶ *q*

   r

   s ⟶ *t*

   not *t*

First subconclusion (using last two premises):

   not *s*

Valid. DC.

Second subconclusion:

   (*q* and *r*) ⟶ *s*

This conclusion must be accepted, since it represents a valid argument, as can be seen in the following diagram:

Third subconclusion (using first and second subconclusions):

   not both *q* and *r*, which is the same as the following: not (*q* and *r*)

Valid. DC.

Fourth subconclusion (using third subconclusion and second premise):

   not *q*

Valid. Affirmation of negajunct.

Final conclusion (using fourth subconclusion and first premise):

   not *p*

Valid. DC.

Note: There are a number of ways this argument could have been handled. The important thing is to have an orderly step-by-step procedure. For an orderly sentence reasoning format see (∴) "Step-by-Step Organization of Arguments" in Chapter 3.

4-77. Let 'p' = 'the piece of wood sinks in the beaker of alcohol'

Let 'q' = 'its specific gravity is greater than one'

Let 'r' = 'anything with a specific gravity greater than one will sink in water'

Let 's' = 'it will sink in water'

Premises:

    $q \longrightarrow p$

    r

    p

Conclusion:

    s

Invalid because the first step, which combines premises 1 and 3, is invalid (AC).

4-78.

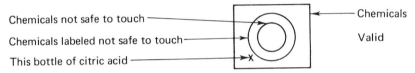

4-79. Let 'p' = 'he is really listening to this music'

Let 'q' = 'his eyes are closed'

Sentence reasoning premises:

    $p \longrightarrow q$

    not q

Sentence reasoning conclusion:

    not p

Valid. DC. Hence we know that Frank is not really listening to this music. Next:

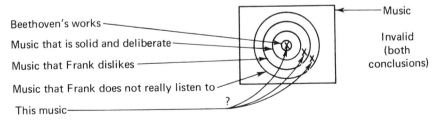

4-80. The strategy that I shall follow here is to reduce the alternation in the third sentence down to coverage of "my room" only, and then to eliminate the alternatives one by one. If the proposed conclusion is the only alternative left, then the argument is valid.

The rooms in Stone Hall

My room

Rooms that either have very dark-colored
walls, or have no windows, or are large,
or are well-lighted

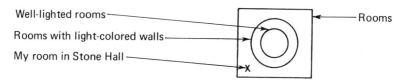

Rooms

1. From the above the following is established: My room either has very dark-
colored walls, or has no windows, or is large, or is well lighted. Next, to
eliminate the last alternative:

Well-lighted rooms

Rooms with light-colored walls

My room in Stone Hall

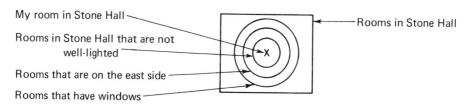

Rooms

2. From this the following is established: My room in Stone Hall is not well
lighted. Next, to eliminate the second alternative:

My room in Stone Hall

Rooms in Stone Hall that are not
well-lighted

Rooms that are on the east side

Rooms that have windows

Rooms in Stone Hall

3. From this the following is established: My room in Stone Hall has windows.
From here we can use only sentence reasoning:
Let 'p' = 'my room has very dark-colored walls'
Let 'q' = 'my room has no windows'
Let 'r' = 'my room is large'
Let 's' = 'my room is well lighted'
Let 't' = 'some of the rooms in Stone Hall are small'
Let 'u' = 'my room in Stone Hall is small'
Premises: p or q or r or s (This is number 1 above)
          not s (This is number 2 above)
          not q (This is number 3 above)
          t
          $t \longrightarrow u$
First interim conclusion: u Valid. AA.
Assuming that a small room is not large, we can on the basis of the first
interim conclusion establish the second interim conclusion: not r
Final conclusion: p Valid. Denial of alternants.

Chapter 5: "Practical Application of Deductive Logic"

5–1. T   **5–2.** T   **5–3.** F   **5–4.** T   **5–5.** F

Index

Affirming the antecedent, 14, 27
  defined, 14
Affirming the consequent, 15, 27, 37
  defined, 15
'All . . . are not. . . .', ambiguity of, 83–84
Alternation, 44–47
  defined, 44
  inclusive, 54–55
  relationship to conditional, 45–46, 54–55
  strong 'or':
    defined, 45–46
    symbolized, 46
  weak 'or', defined, 45–46
'And' (conjunction), 42–43
Anderson, Alan Ross, 119
'Antecedent' defined, 14 (*see also* Affirming the antecedent; Denying the antecedent)
Archimedes' Principle, practical application of, 113–16
'Argument' defined, 8

Beardsley, Monroe, 118
Belnap, Nuel D., Jr., 119
Bennett, Jonathan F., 119
Biconditional, 35–37
  defined, 35

Biconditional (*cont.*)
  symbolized, 36
Black, Max, 118

Carroll, Lewis, 83
Causally necessary and sufficient conditions, 32–33
Circle representation of classes, 66–87
Class reasoning, 11–12, 64–92
  combined with sentence reasoning, 87–90
  contrasted with sentence reasoning, 11–12
  described, 11–12
Class representation by circles, 66–87
Cohen, Morris, 119
Combination of class and sentence reasoning, 87–90
Complex sentences, 51–55
Conditional chain, 37–40
  defined, 38
Conditional reasoning, 11–40
Conditionals:
  material implication interpretation, 59–62
  proving a conditional, 56–57
  relationship to alternation, 45–46, 54–55
  relationship to negajunction, 44, 60–62
  symbolized, 25–28, 34, 36

149

Conjunction, 42–43
'Consequent' defined, 14 (*see also* Affirming the consequent; Denying the consequent)
Context, bearing of, 46, 98–100, 104–5, 107–8, 110–11, 112–13, 115–16
Contrapositive, 19–20
Converse, 19
Copi, Irving, 119
Criteria, emphasis on, 11

Denying the antecedent, 15, 27, 37
    defined, 15
Denying the consequent, 15, 27
    defined, 15
Deductive reasoning:
    defined, 7
    types of, 11–12, 100–2
Double negation, 20

'Either-or' reasoning, 44–47 (*see also* Alternation)
Euler, Leonhard, 66
Euler circle system, 66–87
    background, 66
    invalidity, use in exposure of, 70
    validity test, 68
Expertise, need for in the practical application of deductive logic, 97–100, 107–8, 111, 112, 115–16
Explanation as a context in the practical application of deductive logic, 99, 104, 105, 107, 111, 112
Extent of the predicate class, 84–87

Faris, J. A., 119
Fisk, Milton, 119
'Follows necessarily' defined, 7
Frontier thesis of Frederick Jackson Turner, 95, 102–8

Hypothesis-testing as a context in the practical application of deductive logic, 99, 107, 113

'If', 11–40, 44–46, 54–55, 56–57, 59–62 (*see also* Conditionals)
'If and only if', 35–37
Indirect proof, 55–56

Instantiation, 89–90, 110, 114
    definition, 90

Lewis, C. I., 119
'Logical operators' defined, 42
Looseness of reasoning in practical situations, 93–100
Lyons, David, 94

Material implication, 44, 46, 51, 59–62, 119
Multiple premises:
    conditional chain, 37–40
    Euler circle system, 81–82
    step-by-step organization of arguments, 49–51

Nagel, Ernest, 119
'Necessarily follows' defined, 7
Necessary conditions, 30–33
    causal, 32–33
    truth conditions, 30–32
Negajunction, 43–44, 60–62
    affirming the negajunct, 43
    defined, 43
    denying the negajunct, 44
    relationship to conditional, 44, 60–62
Negation:
    double negation, 20
    Euler circle representation, 71–75
'Not-both', 43–44 (*see also* Negajunction)

Omission of material explained, 6
'Only if', 33–37
'Or', 44–47 (*see also* Alternation)
Order of premises, 18–19
'Ordinary logic', 5
'Other things being equal', 95, 109, 110

Partial exclusion, 79–80 (*see also* 'Some')
Partial inclusion, 76–79 (*see also* 'Some')
Philosophy majors, concerns of, 5
Practical application of deductive logic, 93–117
Prediction as a context in the practical application of deductive logic, 98, 111
Premises (*see also* Multiple premises):
    defined, 8
    false premises, bearing of, 9–10, 99–100
    order of, 18–19

Premises *(cont.)*
  putting an argument in shape, 22–25
  step-by-step organization of arguments,
    49–51
'Probably', 97, 107, 108, 109, 111, 112, 115,
  116
Proving a conditional, 56–57
Psychology of thinking, 10–11
Putting an argument in shape, 22–25

Qualifying terms, use of in the practical
    application of deductive logic, 97,
    107–8, 110, 112, 115, 116
Quine, Willard Van Orman, 119

Retrodiction:
  as a context in the practical application
    of deductive logic, 98, 104, 105, 108
  defined, 98
Russell, Bertrand, 119
Russell, L. J., 119

Salmon, Wesley, 118
Self-teaching from this book, 5–6
Sentence reasoning, 13–63, 87–90
  combined with class reasoning, 87–90
  contrasted with class reasoning, 11–12
Shift from the conclusion back to the
    world of reality (in the practical
    application of deduction), 97–100,
    104–5, 107–8, 112, 115–16
Shift into idealized form (in practical ap-
    plication of deduction), 94–96, 103,
    105–6, 109, 111, 113–14
Smiley, T. J., 119
'Some', 76–80
  ambiguity of, 76
  'at least some', 77–78

'Some' *(cont.)*
  partial inclusion and exclusion, 76–80
  'some, but not all', 78–79
Step-by-step organization of arguments,
    49–51
Strawson, P. F., 60, 119
Sufficient conditions, 30–33
  causal, 32–33
  truth conditions, 30–32
Supply and demand, practical application
    of law, 95, 108–11
Symbolization, 25–28, 36, 46, 52, 55, 79

Toulmin, S., 97
Truth:
  necessary and sufficient conditions, 30–
    33
  tables, 61
  and validity, 9–10, 99–100
Turner, Frederick Jackson, 95, 102–8

'Under normal conditions', 110
Universe of discourse:
  defined, 72–73
  negative and positive transformations,
    use in, 72–75
Urmson, J. O., 97

Vagueness, 98, 110, 115
Validity:
  defined, 8
  Euler circle test, 68
  in the practical application of deductive
    techniques, 96, 104, 106–7, 110, 112,
    114–15
  and truth, 9–10, 99–100

Whitehead, Alfred North, 119
Wright, G. H. von, 101, 119